Sick Religion or Healthy Faith?

Sick Religion or Healthy Faith?

Beliefs and Practices for Healing Christian Communities

Ryan Ahlgrim

Foreword by Lisa Cressman

WIPF & STOCK · Eugene, Oregon

Wipf & Stock
An Imprint of Wipf and Stock Publishers
199 W. 8th Ave., Suite 3
Eugene, OR 97401

www.wipfandstock.com

PAPERBACK ISBN: 978-1-4982-8079-2
HARDCOVER ISBN: 978-1-4982-8081-5

Manufactured in the U.S.A.

Contents

Foreword

I hate reading books like this one. It's so easy to read and understand that my eyes slide right over the words. But then what I've just read suddenly hits me, and I have to stop and go back and ponder it. I hate reading books that make me think in deep and new ways when I wasn't expecting it.

For instance, I had to ponder this idea: a *healthy* faith community. Some would say that's a contradiction in terms. But what if the idea of a healthy faith community isn't a contradiction in terms, but a contradiction in expectations?

Like most people, my expectations of faith communities have been sorely tried! For example, for three of my undergraduate years I lived in my denomination's campus ministry house. About fifteen undergraduate and graduate students from around the world (plus some Central American refugees), representing many Christian persuasions, resided there at any given time. In exchange for work around the adjoining church, we lived rent free.

Many of my hopes and expectations were met there. Our relationships grew so deep that we became not only friends but "a family of choice" who supported one another in debacle or celebration. No question was off the table about the Bible, the church, God, or science in our pursuit of faithful, intellectual honesty. We incorporated our diverse religious perspectives in our prayers together. We cared for people—especially the homeless—even when it was inconvenient and a little scary, and we publicly and actively upheld our common core conviction of justice, especially for the oppressed. Some of the leaders served the community with such selfless integrity, joy, respect, and trustworthiness that I pretended that their faith was my own . . . until it was.

But it wasn't all healthy. Simultaneously, I also experienced that community's ills, and they were just as considerable. Were I to do go into detail, I'm sure that those who believe that a "healthy faith community" is a contradiction in terms would feel bolstered in their conviction! Almost certainly they would shake their heads in wonder that I remained a member of a faith community at all, let alone became an Episcopal priest.

But that is what this all comes down to. This is the heart of the question of whether a healthy faith community is a contradiction in terms or a contradiction of expectations. Simply put, it was not, nor is it, my expectation that a faith community always chooses what is best. It is my hope, to be sure, but it is not my expectation. No community, family, or individual chooses wisely and compassionately every time. My expectation is that people continue to be people even within a faith community. That means that sometimes we choose well, and sometimes we don't.

Then why get involved? Because faith communities are unabashedly in the business of *figuring out* how the Holy can make the most of us. We deliberately, passionately, and unapologetically admit that we can't figure it out by ourselves, that we need God's help, and that even when we accept that help we still make mistakes, sometimes even egregious ones.

What makes a faith community so remarkable is that even when we make our mistakes—even when we make egregious mistakes—we don't throw up our hands in despair, or shake our heads in cynicism, and say the faith community experiment has failed. It is just the opposite. Instead, the mistakes give us the chance to practice forgiveness. We learn to ask for, receive, and offer forgiveness, which keeps us together as a faith community. And then we start over. Together.

This is very hard work, and few faith communities have the will and courage to pursue it. But Ryan Ahlgrim shows us a path. He eloquently and profoundly describes twelve practical, doable characteristics of healthy faith communities. He shows us that a healthy faith community is not a contradiction, but a real possibility that grows out of a healthy faith. Wherever two or three are gathered together, figuring it out, God is in the midst of them.

If "God is in the details," then, thankfully, Pastor Ahlgrim has filled those in.

The Reverend Lisa Cressman, DMin

Founder and steward, Backstory Preaching
December 15, 2015
Missouri City, Texas

Introduction

One could make a strong case that it is time for humanity to get rid of religion.

The sickness in religion is easy to see: suicide bombers, genocide, prejudice, exclusion, reactionary politics; ministers abusing children, repressive rules, inequality, decisions imposed by male hierarchies, secrecy, denial of scientific evidence, erroneous predictions of the end of the world, endless debates, obscure doctrines, immovable bureaucracies, financial scams, cheesy art, thin music, trite trinkets, attention-grabbing gimmicks. The list goes on.

Years ago John Lennon's song "Imagine" invited us to dream. What would life be like if we ignored heaven and focused instead on the here and now? What if we eliminated the national boundaries that divide people and the wars they lead to? What if we were freed from greed and the accumulation of possessions? And what if, among all those other activities and identities that people fight over, we were to rid ourselves of religion? Perhaps, Lennon dreamed, we would finally have a world of peace.

His song is naïve, of course. Even if we were to eliminate all institutions and ideologies we do not like, we would still have the original source of our problems—people. Nevertheless, Lennon's song plucks an enticing chord, and there is more than some truth in it. Surely religion has been one of the causes of human misery.

Given the irrational rituals and poisonous products promoted by some forms of religion, it is not surprising that the ranks of those who count themselves as religiously unaffiliated is growing quickly in the United States, especially among young adults. This group includes atheists and agnostics, but also many people who might be better described as "spiritual but not religious." They believe in some sort of God, perhaps pray or meditate, and honor spiritual values and experiences. But they have lost interest in doctrines and religious institutions.

I sympathize.

Nevertheless, I think many of these people are missing something important about genuine spirituality: community.

We have a biologically built-in need for community. It begins at our birth and continues throughout our lives. We cannot thrive and mature without experiencing mutual love and a sense of belonging. Religion, when functioning properly, brings people together to experience this love and belonging. As a result, we mature emotionally.

In addition, community can accomplish something individuals often cannot: make the world a better place. For social well-being to be improved on a large scale and in a sustained way, we need organized communities of people that are passionately committed to a humane ideal. Community offers coordinated support and strength, as well as guidance and wisdom. Community gives us a plan and the necessary resources to carry it out.

Religion combines the strength of community with our yearning to commune with spiritual transcendence and find ultimate meaning. When religion is working properly, it provides a community of committed seekers who are pursuing mutual love, making a lasting difference, and connecting with the transcendent. As a result, religion has the potential for creating and sustaining humanity's most powerful and needed communities.

Although dysfunctional and destructive religion grabs most of the headlines, it is not what religion is about. Has religion often caused harm? Yes, as has every good thing created or enjoyed by human beings. Eating causes harm when we consume food in the wrong way. Sex causes harm when practiced in the wrong way. Families cause harm when functioning in the wrong way. Is the answer to this harm a rejection of eating, sex, or family life? Or do we instead seek to find healthy expressions of these basic needs and desires?

The answer to destructive religion is not the rejection of religion, but practicing healthy religion. Religion, at its root, is about bringing wholeness. Humanity's brokenness will not be relieved by private meditation or rejecting religion. Our deep social and personal wounds require the aid of a faith that is lived out in a healing community.

But isn't organized religion, with all its structures and rules and committee meetings, stifling to true spirituality? Aren't we more free and mature when not bound by the beliefs, practices, and obligations of a faith community? On the contrary: we are more mature and spiritual—and ultimately more free—when we commit ourselves to the work of a community.

Consider the often dreaded committee meeting. Present will be people with various viewpoints, feelings, and personal goals. So to be successful they will need to listen to each other, care about each other's thoughts and feelings, find common ground, and build a vision together. Then they will need to develop goals, and strategies to meet those goals, followed by divvying up responsibilities to carry out their work. This is all quite spiritual because spirituality, at its root, is about turning over one's life to something greater than oneself. A successful committee meeting subordinates and coordinates the desires of the individuals for a greater common good. This is not easy or glamorous, and usually not very exciting. But as Rabbi David Wolpe says, "Together is harder, but together is better."[1] It is this hard work together that has the potential for changing the world for the better.

I have been a part of Christian faith communities all of my life, and I have helped lead some of those communities for the past thirty-five years. For me, this has been an overwhelmingly profound and positive experience. As the years have gone by, my appreciation for community has increased, and I have become even more convinced that humanity's well-being depends on healthy and healing communities of faith.

I include the faith communities of other religions in that assessment as well; all religions can play a vital role in humanity's well-being. I have read about, experienced, and been enriched by other religious faiths. I have liked some aspects of some religions more than some aspects of the Christian faith. Nevertheless, I remain grounded and sustained by the Christian faith. For me, it is potentially the most healing faith.

My purpose in this book is to advocate for a Christian faith that is healthy. A healthy faith produces healing communities, and healing communities are the key to healing humanity. So I will seek to describe the essential beliefs and practices that form a healthy Christian faith. Any beliefs or practices that do not produce and sustain healthy communities do not merit our commitment and should be discarded. I want to persuade the reader that religion itself is not the problem, and that a healthy Christian faith is at least part of the solution.

In the first chapter I will show how the various communities we belong to form our view of reality, and how it is important that we critique those

1. Wolpe, "Limitations of Being 'Spiritual but Not Religious.'"

communities for their degree of health. To do this, I will suggest twelve characteristics for identifying a healthy religious community.

Next I will explain the essential beliefs and practices of the Christian faith: the biblical story, the way Jesus reveals and reflects God, the wholeness that comes through trusting God, and the practices that nurture trust in God. This will culminate in twelve characteristics of a healing Christian community.

I will then consider the relationship of a healthy Christian faith to other religions, and imagine the ultimate destiny we seek.

Finally, I will explore the mystery of who God is, how we know God through community, and why we may trust in God despite our ongoing questions.

Yes, it is time for humanity to get rid of religion—sick religion. So let us begin with tools to help us separate the healthy from the unhealthy, and then we can build communities of faith that can bring wholeness to all.

1

In the Beginning Was the Community

When I was four years old, my family moved into one of the suburbs of Chicago and my mother wanted to find a church for our family to attend. She wasn't particular about what religious label was on the sign, so long as the congregation was friendly, genuine, and did not teach that her stillborn baby was in hell because he hadn't been baptized. My parents tried a number of churches of various denominations, but my mother found something objectionable with each one—like the church that played organ music during the minister's prayer. She considered that emotionally manipulative.

Eventually my parents visited a small church around the corner from our house. They liked it: the congregation warmly welcomed them, and the minister and his wife seemed genuine. The church belonged to a Christian faith tradition my parents had never heard of, but their former minister said it was "kind of like cousins," which was good enough for my mother. So my family began attending the church.

Or to be more precise, my father attended the worship services, my siblings and I attended Sunday school, and my mother stayed home. The attitude of my parents was that worship services were for adults and Sunday school was for children. So for the next eight years I attended Sunday school on most Sunday mornings (I say "most" because I often skipped so I could stay home and watch cartoons on TV). Sometimes I arrived at the church while the worship service was still in progress, so I would go down into the basement, where the classrooms were, and wait. Above me I could hear the organ swell while the congregation sang hymns of praise. It filled me with a sense of God's majesty. Soon the service above me would end and children would begin streaming into the basement for Sunday school.

During those years I experienced my church as a gentle and safe place. The kids were friendlier than my schoolmates, and the Sunday school teachers were kindly and never threatening. I didn't have to worry about grades or a report card. I simply enjoyed doing crafts and learning Bible stories—and eating ice cream at the annual church social. Fourth grade was especially meaningful because I had a teacher who connected the Bible stories to actual history. He displayed photos of the ruins of biblical cities and showed us replicas of the kinds of coins that were used in those ancient times and places.

When I was twelve, the minister offered a class to prepare youth for the rite of baptism and joining the church. I begged my parents to allow me to join the class. My mother was reluctant. "You're too young. There's so much more for you to learn first about God." I assured her that I already knew all about God. She relented. Several months later I was baptized, thereby becoming an official member of the congregation. I thought to myself, "Now that I'm a member, I should probably begin attending worship services." So I did, but I soon made a disappointing discovery: the worship services were boring. My parents had been right—this was for adults.

Discouraged, I went to the minister and laid out my problem. "Church is boring. I don't know the songs and I'm not getting anything out of the sermons. I like Sunday school a lot better. Would it be all right if I just went to Sunday school and skipped the worship services?"

The minister was unperturbed. "Here's what I suggest you do: hum along for now until you get to know the songs, and then sing them as loudly as you can. When the sermon is being preached, write down on a piece of paper what you think is the main idea. And during 'sharing time,' when people in the congregation get up to say what God has been doing in their lives, you can stand up and share too."

I told the minister I would give it a try for three months, but if worship services didn't get less boring I was going to go back to just attending Sunday school.

Three months later, to my utter surprise, I was enjoying worship services more than I had ever enjoyed Sunday school. I discovered that worshiping God with the congregation is more exhilarating than simply learning about God in Sunday school; my experience of a faith community had been enlarged and enriched.

A year and a half later I fell out of a tree, hit a fence, and shattered my left femur. As I lay in my hospital bed, I felt abandoned by my school friends. Unlike a hospitalization earlier in my childhood, I was not deluged with cards and visitors and phone calls. Other than my immediate family, no one wrote me, no one called, no one visited. I wondered what was wrong with me. Then one evening several youth from the church came to my room. They wished me well and dropped off a stack of get-well cards and letters from everyone in the church's youth group. As I read the letters, tears streamed down my cheeks. I knew where I belonged.

Why do we believe what we believe? Why do we commit ourselves to certain ideals and a way of life? Why do we embrace a particular religious faith, or abandon faith? Why do we become convinced of, or deny, a purpose in our lives? Why do we reject God or put our trust in God?

We often assume that our beliefs are the result of rational examination and private experiences. Certainly these play an important supplementary role. But I would suggest that something else plays a far more fundamental role: community. Our beliefs are largely shaped by our experiences of community.

During my adolescence I realized that if I had been born into a Hindu family I would have likely become Hindu in my religious beliefs. If I had been born into a Catholic family I probably would have turned out to be a Catholic. If I had been brought up by atheists, or by parents who didn't participate in any religion, I would very possibly have made similar choices. What if my parents had decided to attend that congregation with the organ music backing up the minister's prayer instead of the congregation around the corner? I'm sure my religious experience would have been significantly different, and my religious convictions would have turned out differently.

Community forms our convictions. Some people are perhaps born with a stronger or weaker sense of independence, making them more or less receptive toward community involvement and influence; and some people are perhaps born with stronger or weaker transcendent sensibilities, making them more or less inclined toward religious involvement and belief. Nevertheless, we cannot escape the shaping influences of community.

The family that raises us is our first and most important community, shaping our relationships, our trust or distrust of the universe, our rules for living, and many of our most basic assumptions. As we grow, other fundamental communities come along: schools, peer groups, work environments, religious institutions. They contribute further to molding the content of our convictions. Whether we have been passive recipients in these various communities, or have actively chosen and embraced particular communities, or intentionally reacted against them, they have all had their influences on us: helping us see in various categories, process information in various ways, and interpret our lives.

Sometimes different communities teach us different, contradictory ways of approaching life. What we learn at school may be different from what we learn at home. What we learn from our peer group may be different from what we learn in church. When this happens, we become flustered; our model of reality now has parts that don't fit together. We may try to ignore the contradictions by compartmentalizing our beliefs: holding one set of convictions when in one place and another set of convictions when in another place. Another option is to choose between contradictory beliefs, discarding the ones that appear less favorable to us. Or we may try to integrate contradictory convictions in a fresh way.

Whichever community has the deepest emotional hold on our life is the community we are most likely to turn to for testing the claims of other communities. But the more communities we belong to, and the more they differ from each other in their convictions, the greater becomes our capacity to critique all of the communities we are involved in—even our most beloved ones—noting their strengths and weaknesses.

This capacity to critique our communities, including our religious communities, is essential for nurturing a mature, robust, well-functioning faith within a pluralistic society.

I believe in religious communities; I believe in their potential to address the entire constellation of human needs. But to have credibility in our world, and to have positive usefulness, religious communities must be healthy.

Admittedly, there is no objective definition for "healthy" when referring to our spiritual, emotional, and social well-being. Having a normal temperature and normally functioning limbs and organs are good measures for physical health, but how are we to measure mental, spiritual, and social health? Sigmund Freud boiled down human well-being to the ability to love and work, which makes sense to me, but even that minimal definition of health is a social construct; it is what makes sense within a certain culture. Definitions and understandings of health change over time as culture changes. And definitions of what is religious are probably even more fluid! So my aim is not to propose an objectively true and constant definition of a healthy religious community, but to suggest a description that may be persuasive and useful for our culture at this time. Thirty years from now (if not much sooner), I assume my definition of a healthy religious community will be out of date, and others will propose characteristics more fitting for tomorrow's culture.

Let me suggest for consideration twelve characteristics of a healthy religious community:

1. *Holds clear core convictions, often grounded in a foundational story*

2. *Cares for all people and nature*

3. *Aspires to bring a needed benefit to the world*

4. *Provides supportive friendships*

5. *Uses the talents of its members*

6. *Facilitates cooperation and conflict resolution while curbing behavior destructive to the community*

7. *Protects individual conscience*

8. *Fosters personal growth*

9. *Insists on intellectual honesty*

10. *Adheres to transparent, ethical practices*

11. *Offers leadership that serves the community, not itself*

12. *Enables connection with the transcendent*

Holds clear core convictions, often grounded in a foundational story. A family that had left my congregation and joined another church returned to my congregation a few years later. I asked why they had decided to return to our congregation. One of the parents told me, "My son asked me what our church believed, and I realized that after five years of attending there I didn't know the answer. We decided we wanted to raise our children in a church that knows what it believes."

A healthy religious community doesn't need to have a detailed, written set of beliefs, but it does need some clear core convictions. For instance, one church in Washington, DC puts its core convictions this way: "Our one law is to love God and neighbor. We are not concerned about your signing off on a creed. There have always been persons who believed correctly but acted unjustly. Justice matters. . . . We draw the circle of God's love large. . . . Christ is the center here. No one more and nothing less."[1]

Core convictions give a community its identity. They help define what makes this community different from, or similar to, other communities. The mission and purpose of the community flow from these core convictions.

Where do these core convictions come from? Most likely, a foundational story. Though there are exceptions, most religious communities find the grounding of their convictions in one or more sacred stories. So a healthy religious community must know its foundational story and have a compelling interpretation of that story that results in clear core convictions.

Though core convictions are essential for a strong identity and purpose, they are not set in stone; they should be able to be reinterpreted and changed, though not easily. As a community encounters new information and situations, it may alter some core convictions to adapt to a new challenge.

In some Eastern religious traditions, a foundational story may express itself more in the form of rituals rather than in cognitive ideas. An American philosopher once said to a Shinto priest, "We've been now to a good many ceremonies and have seen quite a few shrines. But I don't get your ideology. I don't get your theology." The priest responded, "I think we don't have ideology. We don't have theology. We dance."[2] Core convictions do not have to be restricted to cognitive ideas; they can be articulated through sacred rituals that effectively convey an experienced spiritual reality for that community.

Cares for all people and nature. When the United States invaded Iraq in 2002, initiating the Iraq War, a wave of patriotism swept through virtually all of the churches of America. Bumper stickers and church signs everywhere proclaimed the messages "Support Our Troops," "God Bless America," and "Pray for America." To my congregation, these messages seemed overly constricted in their scope of concern. After all, one of the stated purposes of that war was to free the people of Iraq from the tyranny of its dictator. In addition, it was the people of Iraq who were bearing the brunt of the violence and casualties due to our invasion. So our church sign read, "Pray for Iraq." Someone in the neighborhood must have found our message offensive because our church sign was immediately spray-painted

1. Riverside Baptist Church, http://www.riversidedc.org/about/.
2. Moyers, "Introduction," xx.

and another sign was smashed. Lest we be misunderstood as restricting our concern only to Iraqis, we changed the sign to read, "Also pray for Iraq."

A healthy religious community teaches and practices concern for all human beings, including those who are not members of the community, or who believe differently, or who act differently, or who are perceived as a threat, or who are labeled as enemies. There are indeed people who are a danger to the community, and there are always going to be persons whom the community does not like or whose behavior the community cannot tolerate. Even so, a healthy religious community does not strip those persons of their value as human beings. They still receive the care and concern of the community.

A healthy community extends its care to nature as well. Albert Schweitzer, the famous theologian and missionary doctor, summed up the essence of ethics as "reverence for life." All life and being is interconnected. Our well-being depends on the well-being of the rest of nature.

An unhealthy religious community, on the other hand, ignores concern for nature and divides people into those who deserve our concern and those who do not. Care is restricted to those within the community or those who benefit the community. Value is withheld from those who are different, especially those who may pose a threat to the community. An unhealthy community promotes dividing people into groups of relative worth, nurtures an attitude of hostility to the outsider, and views nature as existing primarily for exploitation.

Aspires to bring a needed benefit to the world. Not every community has the lofty mission of bringing a needed benefit to the world, but religious communities do, or should, because they are by their nature meant to be world-healers—at least in their own little corner of the world. Religion is about addressing humanity's problems through seeking answers in an underlying reality. A faith community that pursues trivial goals, or is focused mostly on institutional maintenance, has lost its purpose and is existing merely for the sake of existing.

So a healthy religious community discerns a genuine need in the world—physical, emotional, spiritual, or all three—and then seeks to fulfill that need through resources available to the community.

Provides supportive friendships. Flocks of geese fly in a V-formation. The reason geese do this is because each flap of a goose's wing creates an uplift for the bird that is behind it, so that geese in a V-formation can travel up to 50 percent farther than on their own. Geese honk as they fly because this encourages the geese ahead of them to keep on going. An ill or wounded goose that falls out of formation will be accompanied by two other geese until it dies or is well enough to fly again.[3]

A healthy religious community operates in a similar fashion. Newcomers to a congregation will normally leave it if they have not made several significant friends within the first few months of attendance. Friendship is a basic need of human life, and a community can hardly be called a community that does not provide this essential emotional support. But for friendships to form there must be opportunity for people to get to know each other and share with each other on a personal level. If a religious community of several hundred people meets only once a week for a large worship service, after which people simply go home, friendships may not develop. There must be smaller settings that encourage sharing and emotional intimacy, such as classes, meals, fellowship groups, project groups, or simply meeting around a coffeepot. The more opportunities there are for building relationships around different activities, the healthier one's network of friends will become.

Friendship, though, is not merely chatting amiably with a familiar person. Friendship in a religious community means that mutual support and encouragement are offered, and that there are people one can rely on in times of need. Together we can do more and endure more than we can alone. Coals in a grill stay hot if they are lumped together, but when they are separated they quickly become cold.

5. *Uses the talents of its members.* The Danish philosopher Soren Kierkegaard once compared the church to a play: there are actors on the stage, a prompter behind the curtain, and an audience. Many churches assume the following roles: the actors are the ministers or musicians, the prompter is God, and the audience is the congregation. But Kierkegaard said that this is all wrong. Instead, the actors are the congregation, the prompter is the minister, and the audience is God.[4]

In a healthy religious community it is the congregation—not a few leaders—who perform the mission of the community. The task of the leaders is to help encourage, discern, and equip members to use their gifts to

3. Widemark, "Lessons from the Geese."
4. Oden, *Parables of Kierkegaard*, 89–90.

enhance the mission of the community. Participating in a healthy religious community is not a spectator sport: it is not watching a clergyperson preach or a music group perform; it is not sitting in a sanctuary waiting to be enriched by someone else's actions. Membership in a religious community means being actively engaged in that community's mission. It means participating in worship or rituals or classes, not for the sake of being fulfilled, but for the sake of being prepared to do the work of that community. Fulfillment comes through using one's talents to enhance the mission of the faith community.

6. *Facilitates cooperation and conflict resolution while curbing behavior destructive to the community.* While I was in seminary being trained to become a minister, a stranger came to campus who began attending classes without enrolling, and then disrupted the classes by shouting at the professors during their lectures. Various students and professors tried to deal kindly with him and reason with him, but his behavior continued. Eventually the seminary learned that this fellow had a long history of mental illness and that it was his habit to go to colleges and seminaries and disrupt classes until the police were called and he was forcibly removed.

The seminary was reluctant to repeat this pattern of relying on the coercive force of the police. Instead the seminary called an assembly of all the students, professors, and administrators to answer the question: what should we do? Since the man would not agree to receive psychiatric help, or to cease his disruptive behavior at the seminary, the consensus was to cease talking to him and to ignore him. A couple days later he left the campus.

I don't know whether that was the most appropriate course of action, but it made me aware of the fact that a community, in order to continue functioning, has to have an effective way of responding to destructive behavior and resolving conflict. A religious community will fall apart if behavior intolerable to its proper functioning is allowed to continue. The behavior does not need to be shocking and highly immoral, such as child molestation or physical abuse; it can be as simple as continually interrupting meetings or calling people names or acting like a bully.

In medieval Europe, if a person believed the wrong things, said the wrong things, or did the wrong things, the religious community might burn the person at the stake. But such ghastly punishment also undermined the religious community, replacing faith with fear, devotion with conformity, and caring with violence. A healthy religious community curbs destructive behavior in nonviolent ways, not only to preserve genuine faith, devotion, and love, but also because religious communities make mistakes. Perhaps the behavior the community thought was intolerable was actually a helpful critique. The ancient Athenians decided they had to put Socrates to death for corrupting the minds of the young; today we consider Socrates the wiser one.

In most cases, a religious community can curb behavior destructive to it through honest communication, gentle persuasion, counseling, and perhaps an accountability plan. In the most extreme cases in which the person causing the disturbance will not discontinue the behavior, the religious community may have to exclude the person from itself.

But there is another type of troublesome behavior that is far more common and inevitable in a religious community: conflict among members. Conflict is natural; it is inevitable that individuals will have different habits, personalities, assumptions, or goals that are not completely compatible with those of others with whom they work and worship. Conflict will sometimes split a religious community, but more often it simply bleeds energy out of the system and replaces a sense of satisfaction with a feeling of resentment. And so it is important that a healthy religious community has mature ways of resolving conflict.

The temptation of most communities is to avoid conflict and try to ignore it. But this simply hides it, and the conflict comes out in hidden ways. The healthy community deals with conflict openly, face to face, between the persons directly involved. Honest sharing, careful listening, ongoing caring, and a search for a mutually satisfying solution are the keys to successful conflict resolution. The goal is not simply to give in to make others happy, or to compromise so that both sides win a little and lose a little. The ideal is to understand each other's underlying concerns so well that a creative solution is found in which all sides truly win.

Not every conflict has a win-win solution, but a healthy community works at it, and finds it more often than not. When a win-win solution is not possible, then members should seek to compromise. Individuals mature not by refusing to cooperate when they disagree, but by bracketing disagreements and personal preferences while working cooperatively for the common good. But if there are persistent winners and losers, the losers will carry resentment and will undermine cooperative efforts. In the long run, either a religious community finds win-win solutions or the community itself will lose.

7. *Protects individual conscience.* Cooperation has limits. As much as cooperation is a vital ingredient for a successful community, cooperation should not go so far as to violate anyone's conscience. A healthy religious community respects and protects those whose conscience will not allow them to cooperate in a particular action of the community. Allowing freedom of conscience helps the faith community see its limitations and imperfections (and perhaps take itself less seriously). The freedom of the individual to express disagreement, and especially to refuse a particular action on the basis of conscience, is part of the ongoing process of the religious community discerning what convictions and purposes are the best and truest for the community.

Not only do disagreements not always have a win-win solution, they do not always have a compromise solution either. When it comes to genuinely held differences about what is morally right, a healthy religious community agrees to disagree, honoring each other's fundamental commitment to doing what is right, and continuing to focus on and celebrate the mission they share.

8. *Fosters personal growth.* I once observed a church that had a wonderful ministry to people who suffered deep emotional wounds. The minister opened the doors of the church to the desperate and damaged, extending unconditional welcome and inclusion. It was amazing for me to see the hope and transformation made possible by simply offering grace to those who thought they were unlovable. But I also noticed something else that troubled me: the congregation treated the minister like a savior, and the minister craved their love and attention. They appeared to be in a relationship of codependency. Predictably, when the minister left the church, the congregation suffered significant collapse.

A healthy faith community challenges its members to grow to greater emotional maturity. That means, among other things, that the leadership does not create a dependent relationship. I remember another minister who told his congregation that the church would not survive without him. The congregation fired him and then, without any minister, experienced new vitality!

But personal growth is about more than avoiding dependent relationships; it means we are encouraged to engage in serious self-examination about our behavior and attitudes. One of the steps in Alcoholics Anonymous is to make a "searching and fearless moral inventory of ourselves." This step is followed by sharing that self-examination with another person, which has the effect of promoting honesty and accountability.

A community that simply entertains us or tries to keep us happy or busy, but does not challenge us or appropriately confront us and foster our growth, will not bring greater healing to the world.

9. *Insists on intellectual honesty.* All religious communities claim to be committed to truth. Indeed, the proclaiming of a particular spiritual truth is often at the core of their convictions and mission. But once a community has arrived at what it believes the truth to be, and has committed itself to that definition of the truth, it always faces the temptation to ignore, discount, or even hide other information that comes along that calls into question the validity of that defined truth. In an unhealthy religious community members are "protected" from contrary information that might disturb their established convictions about what the truth is.

A healthy religious community avoids the temptation of hiding from new and contrary information. As many great religious leaders have said, "All truth is God's truth." If God is ultimate truth, then those devoted to God must not be afraid of any truths, no matter how contrary to our previous convictions and no matter the source. One of the tasks of a healthy community is to integrate all relevant information and truths. The wider the scope of information collected, and the more successfully this information is integrated into the community's convictions and mission, the more intellectually honest and truthful that community becomes.

Such an integration is difficult and never complete. Many religious communities, devoted to incorporating all the truths they can find, end up with a confusing mishmash of ideas without any clear and coherent convictions. A successful integration of broad and diverse information requires developing reasonable criteria for evaluating information, and finding organizing principles (fundamental truths) that make sense of all of the most persuasive information. Truth, in a healthy religious community, is sturdy but flexible. It has been tested by generations of experience as well as by a full array of diverse sources of information. But a healthy religious community has the humility and honesty to stay open to a continuing flow of new information that may, from time to time, require adjusting the community's understanding of truth.

The Bible itself is a good example of this process. Within its pages the concept of God and of God's will shifts and takes on new characteristics over time due to different experiences and new information. The ethical norms of the Bible are not static, but develop in the face of changing circumstances. The result is a dynamic conversation within the Bible that is never fully resolved or synthesized.

Adheres to transparent, ethical practices. I once visited a church in which the worship service concluded with an altar call: the minister invited those who wished to recommit their lives to God to come forward for prayer. A young man sitting next to me stood up and went forward. His girlfriend, who was also sitting near me, expressed excitement at seeing him go forward, assuming he was resolving a spiritual obstacle in his life. After the service was over his girlfriend, full of gleeful expectation, asked him about his recommitment to God. He replied, "I just went forward to help encourage other people to do so."

A healthy religious community does not practice deceit or manipulate its members. By "manipulate" I do not mean appealing to emotions. Emotion and emotionalism can be a legitimate and central aspect of a faith tradition. But sneaky, underhanded methods for motivating people have no place in a healthy system.

A healthy religious community also avoids hidden agendas, hidden processes, and hidden decisions. The organizational structure and functioning of the community should be clear to everyone involved. Decision-making processes should be open, understood, and supported by the community. Whatever programs the community engages in must be conducted with honesty and integrity.

Offers leadership that serves the community, not itself. Examples of religious community leaders acting with self-serving behavior are so common as to need no illustration. We all know or have heard of ministers who have engaged in sexual misconduct, theft, tyrannical decision making, or self-aggrandizement. Leadership in any kind of community always faces the temptation of selfish use of power. It is not a problem peculiar to religious communities. As Lord Acton famously said, "Power tends to corrupt, and absolute power corrupts absolutely."

Within this quote are some of the seeds of the solution. If religious communities do not want their leaders abusing their power so readily, then religious communities need to distribute power, balance power, and make leaders accountable to the community. Faith communities that are led by one person or a small group of persons who control the flow of information and all of the final decisions are ripe for leadership that will eventually serve its own interests. Some religious communities try to solve the problem of leadership power by not having leaders, but I have not seen this work in the long term, and functional leaders always emerge anyway. A better approach, it seems to me, is to have designated leaders who provide initiative and maintain good organization, and groups delegated for detailed decision making, but to have all major decisions made through community discernment and consensus.

In addition to wise structural policies, a healthy religious community nurtures a philosophy of leadership that is focused on service to others. One aspires to leadership not for the sake of power, recognition, future ambitions, or personal benefits, but for the sake of helping the community enhance its mission. In some faith traditions leaders perform essential roles but have no special powers or privileges. I think that best fosters a leadership that serves.

Enables connection with the transcendent. At the heart of religious communities is a relationship to the divine or to some other reality that cannot be fully known through reason alone. It is this relationship that puts fire into the community's mission and enables participants to transcend their self-centered limitations. A religious community that has lost this vital relationship—that no longer appreciates a deeper reality—has nothing special to offer the world.

I believe these twelve characteristics of a healthy religious community may be applied to any religion—Christianity, Buddhism, Islam, etc. Within each religion are congregations that are basically healthy as well those that are unhealthy. The sick ones should be made more healthy or abandoned, because they are doing more harm than good; they are actually undermining whatever mission they claim to have to be a benefit to the world. An unhealthy congregation may grow, attracting thousands, but that does not mean it is healthy. Growth and activity are not always signs of health. Rather, as Jesus said, "You will know them by their fruits" (Matthew 7:16).[5]

5. All Scripture citations are from the New Revised Standard Version unless otherwise noted.

A healthy congregation will produce healthy fruit: mature individuals who are working together, extending care, benefiting the world, and solving problems. A sick congregation tends to produce people who are irresponsible, fearful, resentful, unfocused, dishonest, or discouraged.

It may also be the case that an entire religion, or a certain branch within a religion, is more sick than healthy. I do not have sufficient knowledge of other religions to make a judgment as to which ones, or which branches, may or may not be healthy. But it seems unrealistic to think that all religions are equally good and healthy. Not all governments are equally healthy; not all companies are equally healthy; not all schools are equally healthy; not all families are equally healthy; so I see no reason for believing that all religions and all branches within religions are equally healthy.

However, it is unwise to throw stones, especially when our knowledge of other religious communities is limited. It is wiser for us to examine our own religious communities, or the ones closest at hand, and discern whether they are healthy enough, and healing enough, to persuade us to become involved.

No religious community is perfect. All congregations and denominations will exasperate us or disappoint us from time to time. But one indication that we may nonetheless be in a good place is when life in the community is better than life outside the community. The famous American theologian Reinhold Niebuhr once compared the church to Noah's ark, suggesting that the smell inside would be unbearable if it weren't for the storm outside. My own experience is more positive than this. Despite occasional frustrations and stresses (some severe), I have enjoyed and found deep meaning and healing in every faith community to which I have belonged. Sometimes I have imagined taking a break from church, but I doubt I would find it satisfying for very long. I suspect that a shallow emptiness would drive me back to finding a community that seriously and successfully pursues the good, the true, and the beautiful.

We human beings are always a work in progress—growing, maturing, struggling, working things out. We bring our imperfections into whatever communities we belong to, and so those communities inevitably reflect those imperfections. Even so, together we can agree to practice certain traits or characteristics that will cultivate healthy communities.

I belong to a healthy, healing religious community—or at least it appears that way to me. It is a community within the Christian faith, and I want to nurture more of these communities because I want to help bring more healing to the world. So what are the essential beliefs and practices of the Christian faith, consistent with the characteristics above, which foster life-giving communities? That is the question I hope the rest of this book will answer.

2

A Story to Live By

Once there was a village in which a holy rabbi lived. Whenever the village was threatened by a pogrom, the people would go to the rabbi for his help. He would then walk into the woods to a certain spot, build a fire, and say a prayer, and a miracle would happen that would avert disaster. After the great rabbi died another rabbi took his place. One day the village was threatened again and the people came to the new rabbi for help. The rabbi did not know the spot in the woods; however, he remembered to build the fire and say the prayer—and the miracle happened. Many years later, after that rabbi had been succeeded by another rabbi, a terrible threat once again came upon the village. The rabbi didn't know the spot in the woods and he didn't know how to build the fire; but he did say the prayer, and the miracle happened. Years later another rabbi took his place. When disaster loomed, he did not know the place in the woods, he did not know how to build the fire, and he did not know the prayer. But he told the story, and the miracle happened.[1]

The Christian faith begins with a story. It is a miracle-making sacred story: community created, community shaping, and community sustaining. Not every religion is anchored in a sacred story, but most are, because story is how we order and make sense of reality. Without a grounding story it is hard to find and hold core convictions. The Christian faith story provides this benefit—an essential for healthy religious communities.

The Christian story, in brief outline, goes something like this:

God creates a universe that is fundamentally good, and God gives human beings the task of caring for the earth and living in harmony with each other and creation. But humanity botches the job. Instead of trusting in

---

1. Bausch, *Storytelling*, 15–16. I have used an oral variation.

God's supervision and inspiration, humanity decides it wants to be its own god, making its own decisions for its own interests. Once that happens, everything goes downhill. Before you know it, human beings are lying, envious, blaming each other, and committing murder. The imagination of humanity is selfish and self-destructive. God tries to rectify the problem by starting all over with an ideal, moral family, but the pattern persists. There seems to be no way of bringing healing and harmony to humanity.

So God initiates a long-term plan to resolve humanity's dilemma. God picks out an unremarkable, elderly, childless couple, Abraham and Sarah, and makes them a promise: I will give you descendants as numerous as the stars, and give them a land to live in, and they will become a great community through which I will bless all communities. God persuades Abraham to trust God, and trust binds them together in a holy partnership. After many dangers and disappointments, the couple finally has a son, and through that son other descendants are born, and those descendants have yet further descendants until, after many generations, they become a numerous people.

But now a new problem arises: Those descendants left the land promised to them and have become an enslaved population in Egypt. God must come to their rescue, and does so by sending them a leader, Moses, who goes to the pharaoh of Egypt with a message from God: "Let my people go." God sends plagues on Egypt until the pharaoh finally agrees to release the slaves, but then the pharaoh changes his mind and chases after them with his army of chariots. God blows back the waters of the sea so the slaves can escape, and when pharaoh and his army pursue the waters of the sea surge back and drown them.

Moses leads these former slaves to a mountain, where God gives him a set of laws and sacred agreements for creating a new community that is dedicated to God. After long wandering in the wilderness, their trust and dedication to God tested, the people finally re-enter the land promised to them. They establish a new nation, named Israel, with a unique relationship with God, committed to justice and protection for the poor and powerless.

But the nation of Israel is not always faithful to God. Even its best leaders sometimes make disastrous and selfish decisions. God sends prophets to confront and warn the national leaders to return to the ways of justice, but after several centuries the nation is destroyed by an invading army and many of the leading citizens are carried away into captivity. Nevertheless, God promises not to abandon these people, and sends prophets to tell them that one day their community, led by God's Spirit, will rule the world with peace and justice.

Over time, the descendants of those who were taken away into captivity are able to return to the land, and they rebuild their community on a modest level. Most of the time they are controlled and oppressed by empires much stronger than themselves, but they continue to hope that God will send another leader to rescue them and fulfill the promise that God's community will prevail.

Then a simple carpenter, Jesus of Nazareth, begins traveling from village to village announcing that God's liberating community is now coming into the world, and he invites everyone to believe in its coming and join it. Jesus heals the sick to show that God is defeating the forces of despair and that God's new community is dawning. He extends his hand to the impure and the outcasts, giving inclusion to the rejected and forgiveness to the hopeless. He teaches people to put God's justice above all possessions, comforts, and sources of security—trusting in God alone and letting go of all fear. He urges people to be reconciled with each other and to extend love under all circumstances, even to enemies.

Because Jesus' message of God's emerging community threatens the political and religious order, the authorities arrest him and execute him. His followers are devastated and run away in fear. But soon afterwards his tomb is found empty. He himself appears to his followers, telling them God has raised him to life and that their mission now is to continue his mission: build God's new community, empowered by God's Spirit, and bring healing to humanity.

His followers embrace this mission with newfound courage, and soon they are creating new communities in every nation—breaking down ethnic, religious, social, economic, and gender barriers. All are brought together in mutual love and trust in God through the story of God's self-giving love embodied in Jesus.

This is the story of the Bible—or at least my quick and very inadequate interpretation of it. In addition to being a complex set of stories, the Bible is a collection of laws, songs, proverbs, philosophy, oracles, letters, and visions. It is divided by Christians into two main sections: the Old Testament, which focuses on the story of Israel, and the New Testament, which focuses on the story of Jesus and the church. Binding it all together is an overarching story of God saving humanity from itself through the creation and nurture of an inspired community. The Christian faith revolves around this story and sees itself as the continuation of the story. (Judaism and Islam also see themselves as continuations of at least part of this story.)

Most communities need a story that explains where the community came from, what it is, and where it's going. The story shapes the character of the community and guides its actions. The more compelling the story is, the more strongly the community will bind itself to it. We call such stories foundational stories, or sacred stories, or myths. Such a story conveys the community's sense of unseen truths and the deepest reality. The Bible is the Christian community's sacred story.

But is this story true?

When we ask this question, we often mean, "Did it actually happen?" When a movie begins with the words "Based on a true story," we are being told that at least some of the actions depicted bear some resemblance to what actually happened. So did the story described in the Bible actually happen?

For many of those who grew up within the Christian community, the unspoken assumption may have been "yes." This was my own assumption as a teenager. So imagine my confusion when, as a student in college, I learned that at least some of the events in the Bible are contradicted by archeology. Furthermore, within the Bible itself there are numerous contradictions as it tells its story. Most shocking to me was the discovery that Haggai, one of the prophets of the Bible, incorrectly identified a man named Zerubbabel as the long-awaited savior of God's people. How could a prophet who was wrong on such an important matter still have his prophecies included in the Bible!

During one of my college breaks I went to the ministers of my church and asked them if they knew about these inconsistencies and inaccuracies. They admitted they did. I then asked them why they had never mentioned this in their sermons or classes. One of them replied, "Because it doesn't matter. It doesn't affect the message of the Christian faith."

For a while I was angry with my ministers for not telling me that some of the stories and statements in the Bible are historically inaccurate. I felt deceived. I insisted that my religious faith have intellectual honesty. But as the years have gone by I have seen more clearly the wisdom in their point of view. I still think they should have told me during my teenage years about the historical inaccuracies, but they were also right in focusing on the deeper truths of the Bible. Intellectual honesty is not limited to valuing only historical or scientific information. To ask whether certain stories or details in the Bible are historically accurate is to miss the purpose of its stories and to thwart the most important meaning of the word "true."

The word "true" has different meanings depending on what type of story we're talking about. So let us consider different kinds of stories and what it might mean to say they are true or not true:

Myth. Our society often uses the word "myth" to refer to a statement or belief that is not factual. This is *not* the definition used by those who study stories. Instead, a myth is a story that embodies a community's most basic assumptions and values. Often (but not always) a myth is a supernatural story. Most of us are familiar with Greek, Roman, and Nordic myths, as well as some of the myths of Native Americans, African tribes, and various Asian people groups. These stories are usually not anchored in a particular time, but are timeless. They are filled with unusual and divine activity. Many myths are not historically true, but neither are they mere fictional entertainment. Rather, these stories answer basic questions about human nature, society, morality, and the unseen reality underlying visible reality. Myths give people their worldview—their overarching way of understanding reality—and they do so through symbols and metaphors.

Parable. A parable is a short, fictional story with a moral or spiritual message. It is meant to challenge and alter our perceptions of accepted norms or conventional views of reality. So it sometimes functions as an anti-myth, questioning the adequacy of the prevailing myth.

Fable. A fable is a story with talking animals. Usually it is not as deep or serious as a myth or parable, and it is often humorous. But, like a myth or a parable, a fable makes a point, sometimes with a moral attached to it.

Folktale. A folktale is a popular, fictional story—often involving magic or unusual action—passed on orally in a community for entertainment. Though less serious than the kinds of stories above, it also often has deeper psychological or social meaning and significance than the surface story.

Legend. A legend is a story based on real people or events, but with exaggerations or supernatural actions added in. A legend exaggerates in order to be more entertaining or to give certain people or events more meaning—to make them "larger than life."

Novel. A novel is a fictional story told in a realistic way. Novels explore aspects of human nature or society, partly for entertainment, partly to reveal overlooked truths. A novel is often set in a real time and place, and may even include actual people, but the action is mostly or entirely fictional.

History. History is a story about real people and actual events. Fictional elements are not intentionally added. The goal is to be accurate about what actually happened in the past.

This is not an exhaustive list of the types of stories that exist, but it gives us an idea of the variety that is possible. This list also makes it obvious that "true" has more than one meaning. When we call history "true," we mean that it accurately records events that actually took place. When we say that a novel is "true," we mean that its description of the human condition or character reveals important aspects of our lives. When we say a myth is "true," we mean that it tells social, psychological, or spiritual truths. In fact, a myth tells truths that history cannot tell. History is limited to describing outward events and people, and perhaps making some sense of cause-and-effect relationships. A myth explores the meaning of life and our proper relationship to ultimate reality.

All of the types of stories listed above are ways of telling the truth. Some do it by recording events; some do it through symbolism and metaphor. This does not mean that these stories always succeed in telling the truth. The popular saying "All stories are true, and some actually happened" is not necessarily true. Some stories may seriously distort historical, psychological, social, or spiritual reality.

All stories fall somewhere on a continuum between truth and falsity. For instance, the historian must weigh contrary evidence and decide what most likely happened, and from a chaotic mountain of data must select those bits of information that are most relevant and fit them into a pattern that the historian perceives. The result is inevitably imperfect history: some of the "facts" will likely be wrong and the interpretation of events too narrow. Similarly, some myths may express questionable views of reality—that women are inferior to men, slaves are merely property, or demons inhabit trees and water.

Consider the fictional stories that are told in today's action movies. They often contain a message that I consider false: if we kill all the bad guys the world will be a fine place. The problem with this view is that it is likely to lead to a worse world, not a better one. This view of reality ignores the fact that each of us is a mixture of good and bad, but we all tend to think we are the good guys and those who oppose us are the bad guys. The use of violence to kill all the "bad guys" simply creates hatred and resentment, and also legitimizes violence—keeping cycles of violence going.

All of the types of stories listed above are capable of telling the truth as well as getting the truth wrong. One does not judge truthfulness by whether a story is history or folktale; one judges truthfulness by whether a story reflects the deepest aspects of reality.

So what type of story is the Bible? Among Christians (and scholars) there is disagreement on this question, but I think it is most likely that the Bible contains all of the genres listed above. This should not be surprising since the Bible consists of sixty-six separate documents, composed by different people from different sources and for different purposes over the course of hundreds of years. Let's look at some of the types of stories that may be present in the Bible:

Myth in the Bible. Although many Christians consider the first chapters of Genesis to be history, it makes more sense to me to see the purpose of these chapters as myth. Was the author of Genesis 1 intending to write a scientific and historical description of the creation of the universe? Or was he writing a symbolic account of the creation of the universe in order to tell us truths about God (e.g., God is not nature), humanity (e.g., humans have a purpose given to them by God), and physical reality (e.g., it is good and dependent upon God)? Similarly, are the Garden of Eden and the eating of fruit from the Tree of the Knowledge of Good and Evil (chapters 2 and 3) records of an actual place and event, or are these symbolic ways of saying that humanity is in a broken state because of our desire to be like God? It appears to me that the myth-stories of the Bible are primarily in the opening chapters of Genesis and in some of the Psalms.

I think it is also accurate to say that the entire Bible is myth—both the parts that are historical and the parts that are not—because all of it, as a whole, is meant to convey the Christian community's fundamental understandings of the deepest realities.

Parable in the Bible. Jesus' stories are parables. One of his most famous stories is known as the Good Samaritan. In this story a man, while traveling, is beaten and robbed and left wounded on the side of the road. Two religious people walk by but do not help. Then a member of a heretical group, a Samaritan, comes by and helps the wounded man. He even takes him to a place where he can stay and pays the costs of lodging and recuperation. Is this story true? If we mean did it actually happen, then the answer is probably no. This is a fictional story. But it is also a story that challenges conventional ways of looking at reality. Jesus is challenging his hearers to consider the possibility that even the people whom they spiritually disrespect may actually be the most loving and reflect God.

No one doubts that Jesus' stories are fictional parables, and that these parables contain many spiritual truths. But it may well be that there are other parables in the Bible that have been mistaken by some people as historical stories. One likely candidate is the story of Jonah. This story of a reluctant prophet who successfully converts and saves an enemy city facing doom—and then is mad about it—contains various elements that seem exaggerated, simplified, and timeless. It is not a historical chronicle, nor is it meant to be. It is meant to be a parable that challenges our anger at God's mercy and grace toward our enemies.

Fable in the Bible. In the Book of Numbers, chapter 22, we read the story of Balaam, a foreign prophet hired to curse the Israelites. As he makes his way on a donkey, his donkey sees an angel in the road and refuses to go any farther. Balaam beats his donkey until the donkey tells Balaam about the angel, and Balaam finally realizes that the mission he has been hired to perform is not God's will. This story is probably a fable, not history. The question is not whether God could make a donkey talk (or make Balaam perceive the donkey as talking), but whether it is realistic that Balaam would show no surprise that his donkey is talking. He carries on a conversation with the donkey as if nothing unusual is happening. The world assumed by this story is the world of the fable, where animals can talk and humans converse with them. Does this mean this story is not true? Though I do not think it actually happened, it is making a very serious point (humorously) about human pride causing blindness. Even a donkey can see what a prophet cannot!

Folktale in the Bible. In the Book of Judges there are several chapters devoted to the story of Samson, a man who possesses incredible strength whenever the spirit of God falls on him, and who uses his strength to slaughter great numbers of Philistines, the archenemies of the Israelites. This story looks to me to be a popular folktale. The historical problem with the story is not whether God could give such strength to a human being. Rather, a close reading of the story reveals multiple inconsistencies and nonsensical actions. It appears to be a popular oral story, handed down through the generations, with separate stories that don't fit together very well. To me it has all the earmarks of a folktale. It is possible that someone by the name of Samson actually existed who was a troublemaker to the Philistines, but I think it is also possible that he is a made-up character, like

Hercules. But this does not detract from the truthfulness of the story. The Israelites included this story among their sacred stories because it told them something important about our relationship with God: God's strength in us is undone by our own foolishness.

It is possible that a number of stories in the Bible began as folktales, particularly some of the stories in Genesis. When characters don't act the way real people do, and the action seems exaggerated (like in popular movies), one is justified in wondering whether the story has folktale elements.

Legend in the Bible. To know that something is a legend requires having other historical information that verifies that certain people or events are factual, but that exaggerations have been added. For instance, it may well be a legend that David killed Goliath (1 Samuel 17). There seems to be good evidence, outside the Bible, that David existed and became king of Israel. But in this particular story there is a glaring inconsistency with other stories. After David goes out to fight Goliath in single combat and kills him, the current king of Israel, Saul, wants to meet him. Saul has no idea who this boy is—even though previous stories tell us that David is already a member of Saul's court, playing the harp to ease the king's depressive moods! Besides this inconsistency, another record (2 Samuel 21:19) credits a different Israelite warrior with killing Goliath. The most likely explanation to my mind is that after David became a popular king known for his prowess in battle, a story was created that transferred to him credit for killing Goliath. Nevertheless, the deeper purpose of the story is to show that God's power is in the small who trust in God, not in the large who rely on their great weapons.

The story of the Israelites wandering in the wilderness for forty years before entering the Promised Land certainly has legendary features, since the number of Israelites recorded is far too many to "wander" in the Sinai Peninsula. If they had formed up in a line, they would have easily stretched from Egypt to the land of Canaan five times over! Many other incidents in the Bible probably include legendary features.

Novel in the Bible. There are several detailed and realistic narratives in the Bible that are not corroborated by any other ancient records or archeological evidence. For instance, the story in Genesis of Joseph being sold into slavery by his brothers but eventually becoming the prime minister of Egypt is hard to square with what we know of Egyptian history. The story is probably mostly a novel. Its purpose is to probe more deeply into the foibles and strengths of human character and show how God works through the seemingly random (and unjust) circumstances of life.

The stories of the patriarchs in Genesis (Abraham, Isaac, Jacob, and their wives) might be considered novels (with some popular folktale elements and legends). They are set in real times and places, perhaps reflecting actual movements of clans and tribes, but the details of the stories appear to have fictional origins. Another example of a novel with a historical setting is the Book of Esther. It is set in the court of an actual Persian king, reflecting the real kinds of threats faced by the Jewish people, and is told in a detailed and realistic way. And yet the central character, Queen Esther, appears to be fictional since there is no other historical record of her existence. Similarly, the early chapters in the Book of Daniel are set in actual times and places, with actual historical events forming the background of the story, but the stories themselves appear to be fictional. Their purpose is to analyze the evils of empire and the limits of cooperation.

History in the Bible. Most of the narrative sections of the Bible—from the story of the kings of Israel and Judah, to the fall of Jerusalem, to the return from exile to the rebuilding of the temple, from the stories of Jesus' ministry to the missionary journeys of Paul—have a historical basis. Many of the events and people can be verified by other historical records. The editors of the Old Testament are considered by some scholars to have been the world's first historians: sifting through various ancient documents, records, and stories, putting together a narrative account in which they were attempting to be factually accurate, telling the story of many things that actually happened.

This does not mean that they always achieved accuracy. Through archeology and records from other sources that the Old and New Testament writers did not have available to them, we have evidence that the biblical authors, even when they were attempting to write history, sometimes made mistakes. For instance, the author of the Gospel of Luke almost certainly is wrong about the date of a census "while Quirinius was governor of Syria" (Luke 2:2).

The conventions of history writing are quite different today than in the ancient world. Ancient Greek historians created speeches to reflect the kinds of things a person might have said on a particular occasion rather than what was actually said (since no one was recording at the time). Biblical writers seem to have used this same approach. Additionally, history writing today is more scrupulous about removing inconsistencies and unrealistic human behavior than ancient history writing was. To sum up: modern historians disagree as to how accurate the historical narratives of the Bible are, but the evidence is that the main thread of the story of the Bible reflects many actual events that occurred for the Jewish people.

The Bible does not need to be accurate history in order to be truthful. I once asked a rabbi what events in the Old Testament must actually have happened in order for Judaism to be valid. After giving it some thought, he said, "Nothing." In his opinion, nothing in the Old Testament had to be historical for the religion of Judaism to be true. Not all rabbis would agree with him, and the question of what needs to be historical in order for a community's faith to be valid continues to be debated.

When it comes to the Old Testament, I personally do not think it is crucial that any particular event had to have happened as recorded. However, I think quite a lot of it did actually happen—and I'm glad it did. Because what this tells me is that the community's faith has been tested by real life and real history: slavery, exile, persecutions, defeat, and moving on into the unknown. The historical reality underlying much of the Old Testament thickens the relevance and integrity of the community's faith.

When it comes to the New Testament, the question of history becomes more important, because at the heart of the Christian faith is the claim that God has come to us, and rescues us, through a particular human being who has been vindicated by God: Jesus of Nazareth. So for the Christian faith to be valid, is it necessary that Jesus actually existed? Is it necessary that he was a loving and courageous person? Is it necessary that he was crucified? Is it necessary that God brought him back to life in a transformed way? These critical questions will be examined in the next two chapters. For the moment, let me simply say that the portrait of Jesus in the four Gospels (Matthew, Mark, Luke, and John) is based on a real person.

Although the Jesus story, as well as the biblical story as a whole, is historically grounded, the truthfulness of the Bible is not primarily about history or events. It is about spiritual meanings and realities underneath those events, which neither science nor history is equipped to verify or deny. At the heart of the Bible's truthfulness is whether or not its advocacy for trusting in God is valid. Is God the sustainer of everything? Does God have a purpose for the human race? Is God reaching out to humanity with self-giving love? Does Jesus embody the love and redeeming activity of God? Does God's love overcome our failures and brokenness? History cannot answer these questions. These questions are answered by people who have entered the story and have attempted to live it out in the community of faith.

Billions of people over the course of two thousand years have experienced the Bible and been shaped by the Bible. However, they have not all come to the same conclusion about the nature and truthfulness of the Bible. Christians are sharply divided over the proper way to view the Bible. Four views may be helpful for comparison:

The Bible is God's direct message to us, and so it is a fully truthful and accurate guide for understanding God and doing God's will. This view holds that the Bible was written for the purpose of telling us the truth about God, about how to be reconciled to God, and about how God wants us to live. The authors of the Bible had limited scientific knowledge of the world, and were shaped and influenced by many of the conventions of their cultures; nevertheless, God inspired these writers to see God at work in the human drama and to see how God is saving us from our self-destruction. God guided them to write accurately and truthfully about God's character and will. So the Bible is "the Word of God"—God speaking to us directly through human writers who are reliable when describing the essence of God and how we are to live.

The strength of this view is that it focuses on the true purpose of the Bible, avoiding many pointless debates about science and history in the Bible. It also reflects some of the biblical writers' own views of the nature of sacred scripture.

But one challenge to this view is that the inconsistencies in the Bible are not limited to historical or scientific areas; there are plenty of inconsistencies regarding moral guidance and how the Bible portrays God. For instance, in some parts of the Bible God is portrayed as unchanging and possessing perfect knowledge, while some other parts seem to show God making mistakes or having a change of heart. Genesis portrays God sending a great flood to wipe out almost all life on earth; afterwards God realizes this plan didn't solve the problem of human evil, and so that incredibly violent divine act was apparently useless. Was God unaware that this plan wasn't going to work? Does this story accurately portray the moral goodness of God?

The Bible contains instructions given by God that we would reject today, such as the law to execute a son who strikes or curses his father, or the command to slaughter all the men, women, children, and animals in the

Canaanite towns. Most churches today ignore New Testament instructions forbidding women from teaching men or from talking during the gathering of the faith community. The Bible has contradictory guidance on various issues: divorce, sexual behavior, slavery, swearing oaths, and killing.

Christians attempt to resolve these inconsistencies, and still affirm the total truthfulness of the Bible's theology and ethics, by assigning different teachings for different settings or different times in history. Perhaps some teachings are for our private life, some are for our business life, and some for our political life. Perhaps some teachings were meant for ancient Israel alone, others were just for Jesus' disciples, others are meant for the church today, and others are for all people at all times. Some of these explanations make sense and can be helpful for understanding the complexity of the Bible, but sometimes they violate the intention of the biblical authors. I believe there are some moral and theological inconsistencies in the Bible that simply cannot be harmonized.

If we admit that the biblical authors had cultural limitations that resulted in them making some mistakes about history and science, couldn't they have made mistakes in attempting to understand God and God's will? Is it possible that the same cultural limitations that caused them to believe that the world is flat and that the sun revolves around the earth could have also caused them to believe that slavery is inevitable, that women are to be led by men, and that God hated the Canaanites? The Bible is a powerful, complex, and compelling witness to God and God's will, but I think it is too simple to say that every statement in it is an accurate portrayal of God's will.

The Bible is an inspired dialogue about God that, taken as a whole, authoritatively witnesses to our encounter with God and God's truth. This view is that the Bible was written by human beings who had all the normal limitations imposed on them by their cultures, but who engaged in an ages-long communal dialogue about God's creative and healing activity in the human story and in the world. Rather than saying the Bible itself is the Word of God, this viewpoint sees the Bible as the imperfect but still divinely inspired human witness to the Word of God. The Bible is the unique and most authoritative container for the Word of God.

When the prophets of the Old Testament refer to "the word of the Lord," they are not referring to any written documents. They are referring to God's self-disclosure in history and to what God is revealing to them. In the Bible, "the Word of God" does not refer to the Bible itself, but to God's activity in creating, inspiring, sustaining, guiding, revealing, and rescuing.

All of God's actions and expressions throughout history and throughout the universe are the Word of God.

The Gospel of John makes this particularly clear in its opening lines: "In the beginning was the Word, and the Word was with God and the Word was God. . . . All things came into being through [the Word], and without him not one thing came into being." The Word is not the Bible; rather, the Word represents God's activity; it is God's self-expression. A few lines later the Gospel of John goes on to say, "And the Word became flesh and lived among us." John is referring to Jesus. Jesus is the Word of God because he embodies God's greatest redeeming activity; he is God's most direct self-expression. So it is not the Gospel of John (a written document) that is the Word of God, it is Jesus.

From this perspective, the Bible is a human reflection on the Word of God. The Bible is not a perfect reflection or record of the Word of God, but it is a long and dynamic encounter with God and reflection upon God that enables us to encounter the Word of God and be transformed. Rather than us relying on each verse for direct divine guidance, we look for the overarching themes that get repeated, amplified, and clarified throughout the dialogue of Scripture, and we bring our own God-given reason and experience to the Bible to help us interpret and apply it.

One difficulty with this view is that it leaves us in the position of having to discern what in the Bible may reflect human limitations and what faithfully witnesses to God's timeless truth for us. How are we to determine that? What are the criteria? Different Christian communities have adopted quite different criteria, with widely divergent and conflicting results. The wisest approach is to look for the most overarching themes in the Bible and discern their trajectories to see where they may be going. Perhaps the most fundamental theme in the Bible is love. Its trajectory is to become ever-wider and inclusive. If our understanding of God's will for today violates self-giving love, we can be confident we have misinterpreted the Bible. By making love the trump card in interpreting the Bible, we nurture healthy faith communities that care for all people and nature.

The Bible is simply human wisdom; it does not uniquely reveal God or God's will. According to this view, the Bible is the distillation of two thousand years of human experience and spiritual reflection. It represents some remarkable human wisdom, but it has no unique access to God. We should reject whatever is at odds with our own knowledge, reason, experience, or preference. Its truth is on a par with all the world's great literature, such as that produced by Shakespeare or Homer.

This viewpoint is quite attractive for those who wish to create their own individual, eclectic melding of all religions and philosophy. Its problems are that it makes us the shaper of God rather than God the shaper of us, and it elevates individual experience and discernment above that of the faith community throughout time (often not a very wise course!). It freely discounts the Bible's claims about God and what God is doing, undermining the Bible's use for communal identity and mission.

The Bible is oppressive literature. In contrast to the proponents of the Bible's wisdom are those who believe that the Bible is not very wise or truthful at all. This position points out that the Bible contains material that is oppressive to various groups of people: homosexuals are condemned, women are not treated equally in most of its laws and teachings, slavery is condoned and regulated, non-Jews are discriminated against and are sometimes victims of genocide in the Old Testament, and Jews are often vilified in the New Testament. As a whole, the Bible is out of date, dependent on a worldview and body of knowledge that is no longer tenable or usable. We may pick out a few gems of timeless wisdom here and there, but overall we'd be better off without the Bible—or at least with a radically edited version.

There is validity in many of these criticisms. A close reading of the Bible reveals disturbing aspects that we normally skip over without giving them much thought. And certainly the Bible has been used by many individuals and faith communities throughout history to justify horrific abuses against others: burning supposed witches, pogroms against Jews, and invasions into "the Holy Land." But I think this view overlooks the exquisite and amazing goodness that is at the heart of the biblical story. It overlooks that the abuses committed in the name of the Bible have grown more out of greed, fear, and political strategies than out of an actual encounter with the Bible's message. It overlooks the positive effect the Bible has had, and continues to have, in communities of faith around the world.

These four views do not exhaust all the possible ways of looking at the nature and truthfulness of the Bible, and it is possible to combine different views together. It is possible for a Christian to hold any of these four views of the Bible. However, I do not think it is possible for the Christian faith community to thrive over time if it adopts the last two views. They are too self-centered and individualistic, lying outside a communal encounter with the God-story and presuming an objectivity that doesn't exist. Clear core convictions will not emerge from a community that has an individualistic, take-it-or-leave-it approach to its sacred writings. Christian faith ultimately requires that we submit ourselves to God and to the biblical witness of what God is doing, rather than stand aloof and simply analyze it from the outside. Together, in a communal dialogue, we discern its meaning and application.

The Bible is a story that came into being over the course of many generations. We do not know the authors of most of the books of the Bible. The process by which some books were chosen for the Bible and others rejected is a complicated one. But ultimately, the community of faith chose the books that they experienced as being the most true and that helped them survive and even thrive under the most distressing circumstances.

Because the Bible was composed by many people over many centuries, bringing together various stories and songs and laws and proverbs, it is often inconsistent and unclear, even about God. Most of the Bible was written before the Greek invention of philosophy, and so the Bible lacks clear, logical, consistent descriptions of God and God's will. But the Bible has the advantage of being a story. A story does something crucial that philosophy cannot do: it engages us with characters. God is the central character of the biblical story—sometimes speaking and acting, but often silent or behind the scenes or simply assumed. Since God is the central character we are able to engage God *in a relationship*. Philosophy allows us to *think about* God, but story allows us to *relate to* God. The story of the Bible enables us to become devoted to God and entrust our lives to God.

Is God simply a fictional character created by ancient Jews? That is a shallow way of reading the biblical story. The community that created the Bible experienced God as real, and they used parables and tribal folktales and national stories to explore and understand and reveal God. Some claim there never was an Abraham who had conversations with God, or a Moses who received God's laws written by God's own finger, but behind these stories there is certainly a community of real people exploring the deepest meanings of their experiences. This story bound them together as a community that survived the onslaughts of empires and empowered them to hope for and build a better world. The story they tell is a healing one.

Humanity has generated truly great stories that have shaped every aspect of our consciousness. Christians have experienced that the greatest story of all is the one contained in the Bible. It is the story of God reaching out to rescue us from our own self-destruction in ways beyond what we could ever do for ourselves. It is hopeful while at the same time being thoroughly honest about all the tragedies and limitations of humanity and nature; it contains all the world's goodness and evil as well as a glimpse of a transcendent reality.

The Bible is meant to be a story that we live by. We immerse ourselves in it so that it becomes our story. Because the story of the Bible is the story of a faith community, we cannot fully understand it and experience it unless we are sharing the story with a faith community that is attempting to embody it. The Bible is true (or at least our understanding of it is true) if its story actually heals us. The Bible is not true (or at least our understanding of it is not true) if it fails to heal us.

The Jewish community has often pondered the mystery of why the community of Israel, out of all the families of the earth, was chosen by God to be a special community for blessing all communities. One of the answers given by the ancient rabbis is that God chose the Jews because they were the best storytellers.

3

Jesus of Nazareth

At the center of the New Testament story, and at the heart of the Christian faith, is a carpenter from a tiny village: Jesus of Nazareth. But did Jesus actually exist? If so, did he say and do the things the New Testament claims he said and did? For the Christian faith to be valid and effective, does it matter?

In this chapter I want to cut through some of the silly claims about Jesus made in popular books, movies, and TV specials, and instead present the facts about him as best as historians can determine them. Since a healthy religious community insists on intellectual honesty, a healthy Christian faith must be honest about the historical Jesus.

We live in a world dominated by sensationalist news and a lack of trust in authority, resulting in an odd mixture of cynicism and gullibility. The public frequently believes dubious reports that have little support while discounting serious scholarship and the best evidence. Information about Jesus is a victim of this same trend. As a consequence, many people have the mistaken notion that there is hard evidence that Jesus was married and had children, or that Mary Magdalene was his secret lover, or that he was gay, or that he was a violent revolutionary, or that he survived the crucifixion and moved to the south of France, or that he never lived at all. But here are the facts:

The earliest information about Jesus comes from a series of letters written by a missionary named Paul about twenty years after Jesus' ministry. Paul probably never met Jesus during his ministry, but Paul certainly was well acquainted with Jesus' inner circle of disciples, such as Peter and John. Paul quotes a few sayings of Jesus but doesn't tell us very much about his activities.

For more complete information about what Jesus said and did, our best sources are four books in the New Testament called the Gospels: Matthew, Mark, Luke, and John. ("Gospel" means "good news.") They are the earliest stories of Jesus that we possess, possibly all dating to the last third of the first century. In other words, they were written down within forty to seventy years of the events they describe. The first three Gospels tell the story in similar ways. Because of this, they are called the Synoptic Gospels ("synoptic" being the Greek word for "one view"). John, on the other hand, tells Jesus' story in a very different way, and often with different events.

To what extent are the four Gospels historical—a record of what Jesus actually said and did? How accurate are they?

According to sources going back to the second century, the Gospels were composed by Jesus' original disciples or based directly on their testimony. Matthew was supposed to have been written by one of Jesus' disciples named Matthew; Mark was written by John Mark, a missionary who was an interpreter for Peter, the first leader of the original disciples; Luke was written by a physician named Luke who was a traveling companion of the missionary Paul; John was written by Jesus' disciple John, the son of Zebedee, who refers to himself in his Gospel as "the disciple whom Jesus loved."

But modern analysis of the Gospels has thrown doubt on this ancient tradition. The four Gospels seem to show signs of being stories handed down rather than direct eyewitness testimony, so they may have been written by anonymous persons who brought together collections of sayings and actions of Jesus that had been circulating among the earliest churches. (For convenience I will continue to call the Gospel writers Matthew, Mark, Luke, and John.) This does not mean the Gospels are made-up fictions. They are not novels or folktales; they originate from people's memories of an actual person who had a remarkable ministry.

Luke begins his Gospel with an introduction in which he explains the purpose and method of his writing. He says that many people have written accounts about Jesus, so he decided, "after investigating everything from the very first, to write an orderly account . . . so that you may know the truth concerning the things about which you have been instructed." It is clear that Luke intends to be writing a history about an actual person. I am sure that Matthew, Mark, and John would have also claimed that their Gospels were meant to be history, not fiction.

But that doesn't mean that everything recorded in the four Gospels actually happened, or happened exactly as described. The Gospels don't agree with each other about many things Jesus said and did. Even the Synoptic Gospels, which supposedly have "one view" of Jesus, frequently disagree on certain details. For instance, if we were to take the position that the Gospel of Luke is entirely accurate history, then it would be impossible for the Gospel of Mark to be entirely accurate, and Matthew would be even less so.

But the sharpest discrepancies are between the Synoptic Gospels and the Gospel of John. Here's a list of some of the most obvious differences between the two:

Synoptic Gospels	Gospel of John
Jesus performs exorcisms.	*Jesus performs no exorcisms.*
Jesus tells many parables.	*Jesus tells no parables.*
Jesus announces the kingdom of God.	*Jesus announces eternal life.*
Jesus' focus is trusting in God.	*Jesus' focus is believing in him.*
Jesus makes no divine claims.	*Jesus makes divine claims.*
Jesus speaks in short sayings.	*Jesus delivers speeches.*
Jesus' temple protest is in the last week of his ministry.	*Jesus' temple protest is early in his ministry.*
Jesus' last supper is on Passover.	*Jesus' last supper is the day before Passover.*

Most scholars agree that the Gospel of John is not as historical as the Synoptic Gospels. But his purpose was different: his Gospel is meant to be a meditation on Jesus' timeless identity. This is not just a modern scholarly conclusion; it was recognized in the early church as well. Clement of Alexandria, a church leader of the second century, distinguished John's Gospel from the other three Gospels by calling it a spiritual Gospel. John, more completely than the other Gospels, is a spiritual reflection on the meaning of Jesus. That is why Jesus himself is the focus of all the teaching. John wants to explore and explain Jesus' eternal significance, and he does that by reading the risen Jesus back into the ministry of the earthly Jesus.

The Gospel of John is strongly mythological. This doesn't mean it is untrue; rather, John intends to reveal truths about Jesus that go beyond his earthly ministry—timeless truths that go back to the beginning of the cosmos and on into eternity.

The Synoptic Gospels are more historical, recording the passed-down memories of what Jesus said and did. Nonetheless, they are also mythological: they create foundational stories for shaping the faith community's identity. The Synoptic Gospels aren't merely dispassionate records about a man from the past; they are stories filled with faith in Jesus' unique role and ongoing relationship with God. In addition to telling us about Jesus, they seek to tell us about God and ultimate reality.

For instance, one of the remarkable stories in all four Gospels is the story of Jesus walking on the stormy Sea of Galilee. Did it actually happen? Our answer will depend partly on our understanding of how God interacts with nature. (I will discuss miracles in the next chapter.) But regardless of whether or not we believe Jesus actually walked on top of the waves, the story is filled with deeper, mythological meaning. In the Bible the sea is a symbol for chaos—for un-creation. When God creates the cosmos in the first chapter of Genesis, God begins by separating the primordial waters, imposing order on the chaotic waves. Throughout the Old Testament, God is celebrated as the one who rules over "the deep." Surely the Gospel writers recognized a spiritual layer of meaning when they said that Jesus came to his disciples walking on the water. It is a broad hint to the reader that Jesus embodies the authority and presence of God.

Matthew extends the mythic meaning of this story by telling us that the leader of the disciples, Peter, asks Jesus, "Lord, if it is you, command me to come to you on the water." Jesus tells him to come, so Peter steps out of the boat and begins walking on the water toward Jesus. But then he becomes frightened by the strong wind and begins to sink into the waves. He shouts, "Lord, save me!" Jesus immediately reaches out to him and rescues him, challenging him to have more faith.

It is hard for me to see how Matthew's addition to the story could be historical—not because it is a miracle, but because it isn't mentioned by the other Gospels. If it actually happened, why did the other three Gospels leave it out? It appears to me that Matthew has created a mythic story about Peter: he represents all disciples of Jesus, who, when we trust in Jesus, can walk on the waters of chaos in our lives; but we disciples are fearful, and we need Jesus' presence to keep us from sinking in our fear.

Creating myths out of actual occurrences can happen rapidly—even when eyewitnesses are still around to remember the actual event. One example of this comes from Constantin Brailoiu, an early twentieth-century folklorist in Romania, who came across a story that had moved from a factual incident to a supernatural legend in a short space of time.[1] He came to a village where he heard a ballad sung about a young man who had been bewitched by a jealous mountain fairy who would not allow him to be married to anyone else. Shortly before the young man was to marry a woman in the village, the mountain fairy pushed him over a cliff. Some shepherds found his dead body the next day and brought him back to the village. When his fiancée saw the body of her dead beloved, she sang a song of grief filled with mythic themes.

When Brailoiu investigated the origins of this ballad, he discovered that the event had occurred less than forty years earlier, and that the fiancée of the dead man was still alive. He visited her to hear her version of the story. She told him an ordinary story—though still tragic—about how her fiancé had accidentally fallen off of a cliff, and how he had survived for a short time after having been brought back to the village by some mountaineers. There was no mountain fairy involved, no murder, and no mythic lament sung by the fiancée.

Brailoiu told the villagers what he had been told by the woman herself. They dismissed her version by saying that her memory had been destroyed by grief. They believed their version was what actually happened. Thus, even in the space of a generation, with many of the original witnesses still present, the village had transformed an ordinary tragedy into a legend with mythic meaning.

Might parts of the Gospels represent the same transformation? That would seem possible. So what, then, are the facts about Jesus? Which are the legends that may have been added? Historians have never come to agreement on these questions, and never will. But historians have developed criteria to help sort out what events and teachings have the strongest likelihood of going back to the original Jesus. Following is a sample of some of the criteria many historians use when studying the Gospels:

- *Multiple attestation.* Is a particular event or saying repeated in different sources that aren't dependent on each other?

---

1. Eliade, *Myth of the Eternal Return*, 44–46.

- *Consistency.* Which teachings and actions attributed to Jesus are consistent with each other?

- *Realistic behavior.* Do the people in the accounts act in realistic ways?

- *Non-contradiction.* Do the stories contain internal contradictions, or are they contradicted by other sources?

- *Embarrassment.* Would a particular story or saying have been potentially embarrassing to the church? If so, it is perhaps more likely to have happened.

- *Consistent with crucifixion.* The best established fact about Jesus (based on sources both within and outside the New Testament) is that Jesus was crucified by the Romans. Is a particular story or saying consistent with Jesus being executed for sedition?

Through applying these and other historical criteria to the four Gospels (and Paul's letters in the New Testament), scholars have concluded that many events and teachings of Jesus in the Gospels are historical. Here is a sampling of items that I think most historians would agree are supported by strong evidence:

- Jesus grew up in the village of Nazareth.

- Jesus' mother was named Mary, and he had brothers and sisters (or cousins or step-siblings according to Catholic scholars).

- Jesus was baptized by John the Baptist in the Jordan River.

- Jesus had an itinerant ministry in the villages near Lake Galilee.

- Jesus gathered disciples and chose twelve men for a special role in his ministry.

- Jesus was sometimes accompanied by women followers.

- Jesus was known as a healer and exorcist.

- Jesus followed the laws of Moses, but interpreted some of them in controversial ways.

- Jesus offended some people by eating with social outcasts and healing people on the Sabbath.

- Jesus' family and hometown initially rejected his ministry.

- Jesus often taught in parables and short, metaphorical sayings.

- Jesus taught that God's kingdom was about to be established on earth and was being inaugurated by his ministry.

- Jesus taught trust in God and freedom from worry and possessions.

- Jesus taught non-retaliation and love for one's enemies.

- Jesus taught imitating God's grace, mercy, and forgiveness.

- Jesus conducted a protest in the temple in Jerusalem.

- Jesus ate a final supper with his disciples sometime around Passover.

- Jesus was arrested on the Mount of Olives.

- Jesus' male disciples deserted him.

- Jesus was crucified under the orders of Pontius Pilate, the Roman procurator.

- Some of Jesus' followers were convinced that they experienced Jesus risen from the dead, exalted by God to a new status, and that he had commissioned them to proclaim God's victory over evil.

From this list one can see that the main outline of the Jesus story, and many of the teachings recorded in the Synoptic Gospels, probably go back to Jesus' actual ministry. On the other hand, the Gospels also contain a number of sayings and events that may not go back to Jesus' ministry.

Who is "the real Jesus": the one reconstructed by historians, or the one depicted in the Gospels? To clarify this question, I find it helpful to distinguish between four different Jesuses:

The original Jesus. This is the Jesus who was born at a particular time and place, and lived an unknown number of years in Galilee and the surrounding areas. He thought things, said things, felt things, and did things that were never recorded and we will never know. He had a childhood that we know virtually nothing about. Even after he began his public ministry, most of what he did was never seen, remembered, or recorded. He had a full and complex personality that is unavailable to us.

The remembered Jesus. This is the Jesus who was known to others who remembered him and passed on certain stories about him. They understood him in certain ways and had various opinions about him—sometimes contrary opinions. Their memories of him were affected by their understanding of him. As memories were passed on, especially among those who never knew Jesus personally, they were shaped to some degree by imagination and creative organization. Within a few decades these memories, along with their interpretations, became the backbone of the four Gospels.

The risen Jesus. This is the Jesus who appeared to various people after Jesus' death. This is the Jesus encountered by Paul, who never met the original Jesus. This is the Jesus seen in visions at the right hand of God. This is the Jesus who spoke to Francis of Assisi in the thirteenth century. This is the Jesus that has been experienced by the faith community for two thousand years as a living presence and guiding power.

The historical Jesus. This is the Jesus that is recoverable through the use of historical tools. This is the Jesus about whom we can have a reasonable degree of historical probability. He corresponds with the information about Jesus listed above.

In my view, each of these Jesuses is true, and they are all interrelated. The four Gospels are a combination of the remembered Jesus and the risen Jesus. The Synoptic Gospels contain more of the remembered Jesus than the Gospel of John does, and the Gospel of John is more suffused with the risen Jesus than are the Synoptic Gospels. The historical Jesus is a thin slice of the original Jesus based on pieces of the remembered Jesus found in the Gospels.

Now here is an intriguing question: which Jesus is closer to the original Jesus—the historical Jesus or the Jesus presented by the four Gospels? At first it would seem obvious that the historical Jesus must be closer to the original Jesus because the legends have been removed. But I, along with many scholars today, have come to a different conclusion. Although the goal of the historian is to try to recover as much of the original Jesus as possible, the Synoptic Gospels may well be closer to the original Jesus than is the historical Jesus.

Why is that? Because the historical Jesus is a very thin Jesus, disembodied by the need for high probability and solid evidence. On the other hand, the Jesus of the Synoptic Gospels (and even the Gospel of John) is a more rounded and complete person. All four Gospels capture the charisma of the original Jesus in a way that the historical Jesus never can. Do the Synoptic Gospels contain legends about Jesus? I think so. But they are still closer to what the original Jesus was like than what historians will ever be able to reconstruct with high probability and consensus.

There's an old story about a rabbi who was arrested and put in jail. One of the members of his synagogue went to the magistrate to plead for his release. "You have jailed a holy man," he explained. "He is so holy that people say that he invited a poor stranger into his home, and when the stranger stole the silverware and ran off, the rabbi ran after him saying, 'Don't run—it's yours!'" The magistrate looked down from his high bench and asked cynically, "Do you think that really happened?" The man replied, "No, but people don't tell stories like that about people like you and me."

The Gospels probably contain some stories about Jesus that never actually happened. But they don't tell stories like that about people like you and me. The Gospels capture the soul of the original Jesus, as well as the continuing experience of the risen Jesus. To me, this is "the real Jesus." This is the Jesus who had such a profound effect on the people around him; this is the Jesus that created a new community of faith; this is the Jesus who continues to affect us today. For this reason the Christian community thrives best when it focuses primarily on Jesus as he is presented in the four Gospels, not on the minimal Jesus of a historian's assessment.

So does this mean there is no relevance or value to the historical Jesus? Should the church ignore the insights and reconstructions of the historians? No. The historical Jesus is important to the Christian community for at least three reasons.

First, the historical Jesus assures us that the Jesus of our faith is grounded in a historical reality—that the remembered and risen Jesus is indeed deeply connected to the original Jesus. The Gospel of John proclaims that "the Word became flesh," that the self-expression and creative love of God was embodied in an actual human being. The Christian faith is the assertion that God is reaching out to us, not through a purely symbolic and mythical figure, and not just through psychological or mystical experience, but through a real human being who said and did things that can change the human story and rescue us from our deepest crises. A historically grounded Jesus gives us hope in the most concrete way possible.

Second, whenever historians have sought the historical Jesus, it has helped the faith community refocus on the radical Jesus of the Synoptic Gospels who subverted the status quo and called on his followers to live out a new kind of kingdom on earth: a kingdom of love, justice, reconciliation, and wholeness. Whenever the Christian faith community is tempted to move into either resignation or comfortableness, relying on a spiritual Jesus who will take us out of this world, the historical Jesus brings us back to earth and tells us to love this world, confront its miseries and injustices, and bring healing to it as we trust in God.

Third, the historical Jesus is fully Jewish, thus undermining the anti-Semitism that lurks in some parts of the New Testament and has infected the church for so many centuries. The more we study the historical Jesus, the closer Judaism and Christianity can move toward one another—and that is a good thing.

Some Christians are troubled by historical research concerning Jesus and the Bible because the results sometimes contradict their assumptions and threaten their faith. I empathize with these feelings; I have felt them myself. All of us are resistant to information that may call for rearranging our understanding of our most basic and important beliefs. But a healthy faith community must try to integrate all available truths, or else truth loses its meaning. The process may be stressful, but that is often a necessary part of growth. The study of historical truth—including the historical Jesus—ultimately deepens faith, making it more authentic as well as more useful in the real world.

So the community of faith is strengthened both by the four Gospels and by research into the historical Jesus. Jesus, in his many faces, continues to fire the imagination of those who encounter him, and to inspire the Christian community to follow him in his continuing mission of reconciliation.

4

The Risen Jesus

The Jesus story, which is so foundational for a healthy Christian community, reaches its climax with the story of his resurrection. The man who was crucified has been raised to life by God. He appears to his disciples, commissions them to continue and expand his ministry, and takes his place at the right hand of God. The disciples then organize a community in Jerusalem in which they eat and worship together, share their possessions, meet the needs of everyone who joins their circle, and proclaim to their neighbors that Jesus has been vindicated by God and is now Lord of all. That community then spreads rapidly across the Roman Empire. Soon it includes non-Jews as well as Jews. Within three hundred years the Christian faith has supplanted the traditional Roman religion. It then spreads to every known part of the world, eventually becoming the faith of more people than any other on earth.

Without the message that God raised Jesus to life, I doubt that any of this would have happened. If Jesus had been crucified and buried, never to be heard from again, the memories of his ministry, powerful and unique as they were, likely would have faded as the generations passed. Perhaps the ancient Jewish historian Josephus still would have devoted a paragraph to Jesus; perhaps not. Maybe the Talmud would have preserved some wise sayings from Rabbi Jesus; maybe not. But without the message of Jesus' resurrection, I think it is unlikely that a community devoted to his mission and memory would have endured. The Jesus story would not have been written down, copied, and preserved over the centuries. Instead, Jesus would have been one of the many forgotten prophets in an obscure corner of the world, joining the other billion human beings on this planet who have left no trace of their existence.

The message of Jesus' resurrection continues to be the heartbeat of the Christian faith and community. It is this message that gives evidence that the kingdom of God—the healing communal transformation of the world—has begun; that assures the faith community that Jesus' way of trust and love will ultimately triumph over human evil; that banishes despair in the face of death; that bestows on the community God's spiritual power and presence.

But did God actually raise Jesus from the dead? If this did not actually happen, how does that affect the Christian message and Christian faith?

A number of stories in the Bible probably did not happen, and I have already suggested that the truthfulness of the Christian faith does not depend on the historicity of various events, particularly in the Old Testament. But when it comes to Jesus' ministry, and in particular his resurrection, the claims of faith are much more closely intertwined with what happened in history, and so the question of whether Jesus' resurrection happened will have huge implications for our faith.

Did God raise Jesus to transformed life? Our answer will be heavily influenced by our assumptions of how God interacts with nature. So let me take a moment to consider the subject of miracles.

The biblical story is full of events that we today would call miracles, such as God creating the universe in six days, Noah saving a remnant of humanity and the animal kingdom in an ark during a worldwide flood, God sending plagues on Egypt and splitting the waters of the Red Sea so the Israelites could escape, Joshua marching the Israelites around Jericho with trumpets and shouting until the walls tumbled down, a virgin giving birth to a child, and Jesus stilling a storm and giving sight to a man born blind. Miraculous stories abound in the Bible. Did they all happen? Did none happen? Did some happen? If some or all happened, were they natural or supernatural occurrences?

For centuries science has been dedicated to finding natural causes for observable events, and mathematically describing the workings of nature through what we commonly call "laws of nature." Science has been phenomenally successful in this quest. So if miracles are defined as supernatural acts that violate the laws of nature, then science is incapable of recognizing miracles. From a strictly scientific point of view, none of the miracles in the Bible actually happened, or what happened must have had a natural explanation.

For instance, when the Bible says God sent plagues of frogs and locusts against Egypt, science would say it either didn't happen or it was a natural phenomenon. When Exodus says the sea parted to allow the Hebrew slaves to escape the Egyptian army, it's either a symbolic story or a mistranslated story, or perhaps a strong wind blew back shallow water in a marshy area. When the Gospels say Jesus healed people and performed exorcisms, the healings either didn't happen or people found relief through natural processes such as the power of suggestion. According to science, Jesus didn't still any storms. Jesus' resurrection? From a scientific viewpoint, it simply didn't happen. This is a common way for many people today to understand the miracles in the Bible.

Another view is also popular: God, from time to time, intervenes in nature. This does not invalidate science or the laws of nature; it simply means that God, as the creator and sustainer of nature, can suspend the laws of nature whenever God chooses. Ordinarily, God does not intervene in a supernatural way; God set up the universe to operate through natural laws and this process is good and necessary. But on rare (or maybe not so rare) occasions, in order to reveal God's self in a special way, or in order to accomplish a decisive change in the human story, or in answer to prayer, God operates in a more direct fashion that bypasses or intensifies the normal processes of nature.

This view allows for the miracles in the Bible to have actually happened. A person who adopts this perspective does not necessarily believe that every miracle in the Bible is historical. Such a person may believe that some biblical miracles are best understood as metaphors. The point is that they *could have happened* even if some did not. For instance, in Jewish tradition there are many miracles attributed to the great mystical rabbi Baal Shem Tov. The tradition affirms the reality of miracles without requiring everyone to believe they all happened. As the tradition says, "Whoever believes all the miracle stories about the Baal Shem Tov is a fool, but whoever denies that he could have done them is a heretic."[1]

Let me suggest yet a third way of looking at miracles. The Bible does not define miracles as violations of the laws of nature. Rather, they are "signs" or "wonders" that reveal the rescuing care of God. The biblical authors could not have defined miracles as violations of the laws of nature because the laws of nature were unknown to the ancient authors. Instead, they observed that nature has fairly predictable regularities, but sometimes

1. Buxham, *Light and Fire of the Baal Shem Tov*, 5.

surprising and unexpected things happen, and even ordinary events (such as a baby's birth) can be a source of wonder. The events of life and the workings of nature—both the ordinary and the unexpected—called for spiritual interpretation. What does it all mean? How is God working among us through these events? So the biblical authors saw the movement and involvement of God in both the ordinary and the extraordinary.

Science and faith are both in the business of interpreting events, but they do it in different ways, looking from different angles; and both, it seems to me, are valid. Science interprets events by asking: what are the natural causes behind these events? Biblical writers interpret events by asking: what do these events reveal to us about God's relationship with us?

For instance, when Jesus healed people, some interpreted it as meaning that the power of God was at work through him, but others interpreted it as the deceptive power of the devil. Whether or not the healings involved natural causation was beside the point. What mattered was properly understanding the meaning of the healings. Events are not simply events; we humans are always looking for meanings in events—meanings that go beyond questions of natural causation.

So what happens if a seemingly impossible event occurs? Faith and science are likely to interpret that event in two very different ways. For instance, what if, while typing this book, I fall into a coma. A week goes by and the doctors tell my wife I have no brain activity and there is no hope. But just before they pull the plug I suddenly come out of my coma, become fully functional again, and have a new idea for completing this book. I am apt to interpret such an event as a sign from God, giving me inspiration for this book.

However, a scientist observing the same amazing event will conclude—as a scientist—that there must be a natural explanation for how I recovered from this seemingly hopeless condition. Perhaps something was missed or mistaken in the tests, or perhaps future research on the brain will throw light on what is for now a natural occurrence without an explanation. May it be that both interpretations are correct? Perhaps God is giving me a sign, and perhaps there is a currently unknown natural explanation. In other words, the event is not a supernatural intervention breaking the laws of nature, but it still may be a "wonder" for me from God.

There are many examples of well-documented events that science cannot currently explain. This does not mean there is no possible natural explanation; it means nature contains elements and processes science cannot yet see—and perhaps will never be able to see. As the early church theologian Augustine wrote, "A miracle, therefore, happens not contrary to nature, but contrary to what we know as nature."[2] If we follow the logic of Augustine's statement, Jesus' resurrection is not contrary to nature, but only contrary to what we know about nature. For God, Jesus' resurrection is an entirely natural occurrence; it fits within the structure of reality God has created for us to live in; it is an event that fulfills the unfolding of nature. But it may never be understood scientifically because of the limits of science's methods.

We can push Augustine's insight one step further. Biblically speaking, a miracle is any event—whether it has a readily available natural explanation or not—that, for the believer, reveals God's involvement with us. The frogs and locusts that plagued Egypt may have had a totally natural and knowable explanation *and* have been a sign to the Hebrews that God desired freedom for the oppressed. The healings of Jesus may sometimes have been psychosomatic or the overcoming of social psychosis *and* been signs that God's kingdom is emerging in our world. Indeed, if God is sustaining all of nature at all times, if all of existence is dependent on God, then God is at work through all of nature's workings, and *everything* is a wonder and sign from God.

For me, God raising Jesus from the dead is a sign from God as well as a possible real occurrence. If it happened, it does not represent a breaking of the laws of nature, but a working out of nature that is deeper than science can see. Deciding whether it actually happened depends not on science, but on the nature of the records, our experience, our reason, and our faith.

So, did God actually raise Jesus from the dead, transforming him into something new and eternal? Let us begin by looking at the earliest account of Jesus' resurrection that we possess: the testimony of the apostle Paul in his first letter to the Christians in Corinth, written around the year 53, about twenty years after the events it describes:

> For I handed on to you as of first importance what I in turn had received: that Christ died for our sins in accordance with the scriptures, and that he was buried, and that he was raised on the third day in accordance with the scriptures, and that he appeared to Cephas, then to the twelve. Then he appeared to more than five hundred brothers and sisters at one time, most of whom are still alive, though some have died. Then he appeared to James, then to

2. Augustine, *De civitate Dei* 21.8.

all the apostles. Last of all, as to one untimely born, he appeared also to me. (1 Corinthians 15:3–8)

For historians of ancient history, sources don't get any better than this. Paul is speaking of his own experience, as well as describing the experience of those whom he knows personally. He tells us in another letter (Galatians) that three years after his own experience of the risen Jesus he stayed with Peter, the first leader of the church, for fifteen days. It seems likely that it was during this visit that Paul learned this account. So the source of his information is probably direct and extremely early—perhaps no more than a half-dozen years after the events it describes.

Paul says that Jesus appeared to Peter (Cephas), then to the twelve disciples, then to five hundred followers at one time, then to Jesus' brother (James), then to "all the apostles," and then lastly to himself. From this list it is clear that the experience of the risen Jesus happened to many people over the course of time, and that Paul probably views himself as being the last to have this experience. He refers to himself as "untimely born" (more literally, "aborted"). This could mean that his experience was more extreme or violent than the others', or that his experience came at a later point in time than the others'. Based on the later account in Acts of the Apostles, most historians have assumed that Paul's experience came perhaps three years later than the others', which may explain why Paul needed to argue so strenuously in his letters that he was a real apostle (one who had seen, and been sent by, the risen Jesus).

What exactly did Paul and the other apostles experience? Paul says Jesus "appeared" to them. Does this mean they saw him within ordinary reality, or they had a vision of him in heaven or on earth, or does it mean something else? It's impossible to say for certain from this account.

The author of the Letter to the Hebrews, the author of Acts, and Paul himself all talk about Jesus being exalted "at the right hand of God." How would they conclude this unless someone "saw" this, and how could this be seen except in a vision? A story in Acts asserts that Stephen, a member of the earliest church in Jerusalem, had a vision just before being stoned to death: "he gazed into heaven and saw the glory of God and Jesus standing at the right hand of God" (Acts 7:55). So it seems possible that at least some of the experiences of the risen Jesus could have been in the form of visions.

Paul gives us another account of his own experience in his letter to the Christians in Galatia. There he says that his message was not given to him by any human being, "but I received it through a revelation of Jesus

Christ." He then goes on to say that "God, who had set me apart before I was born and called me through his grace, was pleased to reveal his Son to me" (Galatians 1:12, 15–16). This does not sound like a physical encounter; it sounds more like a vision or some other extraordinary spiritual insight.

Whatever his experience was, it included receiving a commission and a message, "so that I might proclaim him among the Gentiles" (verse 16). In all likelihood, everyone on Paul's list who saw the risen Jesus also received a commission and a message. Paul uses the word "apostle," which means "sent one," to refer to all of those who have seen the risen Jesus. In other words, those who saw the risen Jesus were also sent by Jesus. At the center of the experience of the risen Jesus was a calling to go and proclaim a message. So, whatever the experience of the risen Jesus was for Paul and the other apostles, it was not simply "seeing" Jesus alive again; it involved a realization that Jesus was exalted by God, and it included a commission to go and tell this good news.

Paul was not originally a disciple of Jesus. Indeed, he tells us that when the disciples began proclaiming that Jesus was raised and exalted by God, he tried to violently stamp out the movement. He rejected the idea that Jesus could be God's special savior and king. But then "God was pleased to reveal his Son to me." After that he fearlessly promoted the message that Jesus is Lord of all, and he started communities of believers all over the Roman Empire who lived out new relationships of love, spiritual equality, sharing, and reconciliation. He was often beaten and imprisoned, but that never shook his resolve and his hope. Eventually he was sent to Rome for trial and was beheaded.

James, the brother of Jesus, was also not originally a disciple of Jesus. According to the Gospel of Mark, Jesus' mother and his siblings thought Jesus was unhinged and tried to stop his ministry. But sometime after Jesus' crucifixion his brother James experienced Jesus as risen and exalted, and soon James became the leader of the new faith community in Jerusalem. Because of his faith political leaders in Jerusalem eventually had him stoned to death.

Peter ran away when Jesus was arrested, and when he was recognized as a disciple he denied knowing Jesus. But soon after Jesus' crucifixion he was apparently the first disciple to experience Jesus alive and exalted. He subsequently gave leadership to the first community of Jesus' followers, and traveled extensively, expanding the movement. According to early tradition, and perhaps some archeological evidence, he was executed in Rome during Nero's persecution of Christians.

These, and others who experienced the risen Jesus, changed their minds, changed their lives, and ultimately died for their faith. Though we may not know precisely what that experience was, we cannot doubt that for them it was utterly real—more real than the shabby world of politics, prisons, and empire. This much we can deduce with a high level of probability: this experience, whatever it was, actually happened to them.

Now let us turn to the accounts of Jesus' resurrection in the four Gospels. Unlike Paul's account, we may not be dealing with authors who experienced this for themselves, or who personally knew those who had the experience. More likely, the Gospels were written by believers who were recording oral stories that had been passed down in the community of faith for several decades. But whereas Paul gives us a list of people who saw the risen Jesus, the Gospels tell us elaborate stories of women finding his empty tomb and seeing angels, and Jesus appearing to and talking with a variety of his disciples in various locations.

As I've already noted, the four Gospels are not entirely consistent with one another when they tell the Jesus story. But their disagreements increase and are greatest when it comes to recounting the events of Jesus' resurrection. Here are some of the inconsistencies:

- The list of women who go to the tomb is different in each of the Gospels.

- The number and position of the angels at the tomb are different in each of the Gospels.

- In Mark and Luke the women do not see Jesus; in Matthew two do; in John only one does.

- In John Jesus tells Mary she must not hold on to him, but Matthew says two women (both named Mary) hold on to his feet.

- Only Matthew says there were guards stationed at the tomb; there are none present in the other Gospels.

- John says that Jesus gave the Holy Spirit to his disciples on the first night of the resurrection, while Acts says it was seven weeks later.

- Only the author of Luke and Acts includes a visual ascension of Jesus into heaven, but the author is inconsistent as to when it happened: the first night after the resurrection or forty days later.

In addition to these inconsistencies there are story elements that do not readily make historical sense: How are the women planning to get inside the tomb to anoint Jesus' corpse? Why does Mary Magdalene converse with angels as if this were normal? How is it that the guards do not become believers when they see an angel open the tomb? Since Jesus' burial clothes are found in the tomb, how is it that he is clothed when he makes his appearances?

But the biggest contradiction is the location of Jesus' initial appearance to the disciples. Mark anticipates it will be in Galilee, and Matthew agrees that's where it happened. Luke says that the appearance was that night in Jerusalem, and John agrees. Luke insists that all of the appearances had to be in Jerusalem. This contradicts not only Mark and Matthew, but also John, who recounts a later appearance in Galilee.

This inconsistency about where Jesus appeared to his core disciples is impossible to reconcile. Either the disciples went to Galilee to meet the risen Jesus for the first time, or Jesus appeared to them only in Jerusalem, or (according to John) Jesus first appeared to them in Jerusalem and then later to some of them in Galilee (though at the shore of the Sea of Galilee, not on a mountain as Matthew says).

When it comes to recording the events following Jesus' resurrection, the four Gospels agree on only two points: (1) Mary Magdalene went to the tomb on Sunday morning and found it empty, and (2) the male disciples encountered the risen Jesus.

The discrepancies among the Gospel writers are so abundant at every turn that it is clear that these stories, in their present form, are more about the *meaning* of Jesus' resurrection than about accurate historical records of his resurrection. When we read the Easter accounts we are entering a deeply moving exploration of what Jesus' resurrection is all about. These stories are reaching for truth that history writing, by itself, cannot touch.

How does Paul's testimony compare with the Gospel narratives? Let's take Paul's list one appearance at a time:

- *Cephas.* Luke agrees that Jesus appeared to Peter, perhaps first, but does not tell the story. Remarkably, none of the Gospels tells this story.

- *The Twelve.* Paul's testimony could fit with either Mark and Matthew on the one hand, or Luke and John on the other, but not with all four.

- *Five hundred brothers and sisters.* There is no account in the Gospels that corresponds with Paul on this point, which is remarkable given the size of the event. It's possible that there is a dim reflection of this mass appearance in Luke's Pentecost account in Acts 2, but if so Luke has fundamentally altered the story.

- *James.* The Gospels say nothing about an appearance to Jesus' brother.

- *All the apostles.* This seems to be a catch-all for including everyone else who claimed to have seen the risen Jesus. It would apparently include apostles mentioned in Paul's letters, such as Apollos, Andronicus, and Junia. The Gospels say nothing about such appearances.

- *Paul.* Luke narrates the story of Paul's encounter in Acts of the Apostles, but clearly does not think of it as fitting into the category of the appearances to the original disciples.

It is also noteworthy which appearances in the Gospels are not mentioned by Paul: to women at the tomb, to two disciples going to Emmaus (in Luke), and to seven disciples at the Sea of Galilee (in John).

The only point that Paul and the four Gospels all agree upon is that Jesus appeared, at least on one occasion, to the inner group of twelve (or eleven) disciples. This appearance, which all of our sources agree upon, presumably contained a message, and a commission to share it.

There is perhaps one other piece of information that the Gospels and Paul agree upon. The Gospels all agree that the tomb in which Jesus was buried was empty on Sunday morning. Paul doesn't say anything about a tomb, but he does say that Jesus "was buried, and that he was raised on the third day." This is significant because it means that both Paul and the Gospel writers thought of Jesus' resurrection as a rising from the grave, not as simply his disembodied spirit going to heaven while his corpse decayed on earth.

Whether Jesus' grave was actually empty, or how it came to be empty, cannot be determined by historical analysis. But because Paul and the Gospel writers understood Jesus' resurrection to be a bodily resurrection, they interpreted his resurrection to mean that the transformation of creation had begun, inaugurating a new age.

Most Jews at the time of Jesus were hoping for future resurrection, not spiritual immortality. Judaism has always been concerned primarily about this world, not heaven. The true home of human beings is not a disembodied existence in an immaterial, spiritualized heaven; rather, our true home is this world—but this world transformed. So it is this world that must be healed; it is this world that must be infused with the presence of heaven. The kingdom of God, awaited by Jews and announced by Jesus, is not heaven, but heaven come to earth. It is the healing and restoration of the world.

Resurrection is an integral part of that hope. Ancient Jews hoped that at the coming of God's kingdom all those who had been faithful to God would be brought back to life (or perhaps more accurately, re-created) to live a fulfilled, eternal life on a renewed earth. The Jewish hope for life after death is a life more real, more embodied than what we experience now. It is a hope for justice to be done, for right to prevail over wrong; it is a hope for a restored community.

What Paul and the Gospel authors were convinced of was that God had begun this restoration in Jesus. The resurrection of Jesus is not meant to be an assurance that Jesus' soul is now safely in heaven, or that his followers will all go to heaven when they die; rather, it is an assurance that God has begun the re-creation of our world, and that we can join in that re-creation process.

If some of Jesus' disciples had seen a ghostly apparition of Jesus after his death, they would have concluded that Jesus' spirit was either wandering the earth or had perhaps gone to heaven; but it would not have meant anything uniquely important. Whatever it was that the disciples experienced—an empty tomb, a vision, a calling, a physical encounter— it convinced them that the kingdom of God is now indeed dawning on earth, and Jesus is Lord of this new world coming.

Believing in Jesus' Resurrection

Whether the experiences of the first disciples were visions, or a physical reality that could have been photographed, or something else entirely, I do not think we can know by historical or scientific means. If God transformed Jesus, bringing him back to life to begin a new age of healing and re-creation, then we are dealing with an event that fits into no scientific category and is therefore not available for scientific explanation. (On the other hand, if our view of reality is limited to current scientific categories, then we cannot believe in a literal resurrection of Jesus.) What we can historically know with high probability is that Peter and the inner circle of disciples (and later James, Paul, and others) had a convincing experience that God had re-created Jesus and given them a mission.

But do we believe God raised Jesus? Do we believe God has begun the new creation through Jesus and made him Lord of all? Do we believe that God's kingdom of trust, hope, love, and reconciliation is prevailing over the kingdoms of violence, fear, power hunger, and brokenness? Do we believe that for all who join God's kingdom death is not our final end? If so, why do we believe?

Some people believe because they have grown up in a faith community that has always taught it. They believe because their culture believes, or their authority figures believe. It is an inherited faith that fits comfortably.

Some people believe because they want to believe. It represents such good news, the implications are so positive, that, in the face of a tragic world in which only death is certain, they believe because it gives life needed hope.

Some people believe because they think the historical evidence is persuasive. They have sifted through the testimony of Paul and the stories of the four Gospels, and have come to the conclusion that something like this must have happened and God is at work within it.

But let me suggest another basis for faith in God raising Jesus. Consider a story told by Luke about two disciples walking from Jerusalem to Emmaus on the Sunday after Jesus' crucifixion. Their hearts are heavy. The one they had put their hopes in has been executed in the most humiliating way. The world's story has once again ended in tragedy. But then a stranger joins them on their journey, and through the use of Scripture he helps them to see that God's story is a repeated pattern of God bringing new life out of suffering, death, and despair. When they reach Emmaus the disciples invite the stranger to have dinner with them. He blesses the bread, breaks it, and shares it with them. In that moment they recognize Jesus and he vanishes from their sight, and now they realize he was with them all along.

Through this story Luke gives us a picture of how faith in Jesus' resurrection happens. Scripture—God's sacred story—shapes us and enables us to see deeper truths than what this world of selfishness and futility shows us. God's relentless story of hope overcoming tragedy prepares us for meeting the risen Jesus. Then, in the experience of breaking bread together—of being a community of reconciliation and hope that demonstrates God's kingdom in the world—we realize Jesus is among us.

The people in the ancient world who joined the Christian movement, who believed that God had raised Jesus to life, did so not primarily because of the testimony of the apostles (especially after the apostles had died), but because of their own experience of hope within the Christian community of faith. Within this new faith community they experienced Jesus' power of healing, Jesus' power of sharing possessions, Jesus' power to cast out the demons of humanity's insanity, Jesus' power to release captives of prejudice and isolation, Jesus' power to love and redeem even enemies, Jesus' power to see a new world dawning, Jesus' power to proclaim good news, and Jesus' power to trust in God.

This continues to be the essential source of the Christian community's faith that God has raised Jesus. In the Gospel stories of the risen Jesus meeting his disciples, and in Paul's letters expressing his extraordinary faith, we find our own experiences reflected. We too experience the living Jesus among us.

Three of the Gospel narratives contain the motif of the risen Jesus initially not being recognized: Mary Magdalene at the tomb, the two disciples going to Emmaus, and seven disciples at the shore of the Sea of Galilee. Each of these stories acknowledges that Jesus is with us as one unseen. Recognition of his presence comes through an experience—our name spoken in love, our nets filled up, food provided. Every life-giving experience of Christian community is a revelation of sharing a meal with the risen Jesus.

But what if God did not actually raise Jesus—what would be the implications? What if the disciples had a purely subjective experience and that Jesus is no longer alive outside our imagination? What if the stories of Jesus' resurrection are powerful parables telling us that courage and goodness and love cannot be stopped, but Jesus' corpse deteriorated like anyone else's and God did not re-create him or transform him into a living presence? Does it matter?

Some would say it does not matter. After all, the stories continue to be powerful motivations for hope, and the Christian community can continue to share and experience God's love and healing.

But if Jesus is actually dead I think we are driven to bad news, not good news. For instance, if Jesus is dead then what is to keep us from concluding that he was a failure? If Jesus' life ended in crucifixion then, from a historical point of view, one should reasonably conclude that the story of Jesus is of a compassionate, sometimes confrontational visionary who was too naïve to realize how the world actually works. Perhaps as he was being crucified, seeing that God did not rescue him and the kingdom did not come, he died disillusioned, his dreams shattered on a cross. In that case his last words might well have been something like what Matthew (27:46) and Mark (15:34) record: "My God, my God, why have you forsaken me?"

If this is the end of the original Jesus, then why would we follow him? Why believe that his way is going to change anything? Yes, some of his teachings could still be inspirational for us, but his central teaching of God's dawning kingdom and trusting in God alone would have been shown to be futile. A sensible person would then find a compromise with the ways of the world.

On the other hand, one might choose to still follow Jesus—even if he's dead—in order to try to prove him right after all. Jesus' example of radical trust and love may inspire us to continue his mission. Many other heroes have died in their attempts to do something great, but that doesn't mean we dismiss them as naïve failures. Maybe we can ultimately succeed where Jesus failed. Maybe history will vindicate him as being the one who saw and lived the truth most clearly. Indeed, that would be one way of reading the history of the church: because his followers through the centuries refused to think of him as a dead failure, they went out to prove him right, and through great faith and sacrifice they have accomplished much good for the world.

This, however, is quite different from the Christian faith and the message of Jesus. Jesus' hope was in God, not our heroic efforts. Jesus trusted in the coming of God's kingdom, not our kingdom. Faith in Jesus' re-creation means faith in God, not ourselves. Furthermore, if Jesus is dead then the heroic efforts of Christians are still most likely based on delusional assumptions. If Jesus is dead then we lose the most important sign that God is bringing about God's kingdom of reconciliation and peace. If Jesus is dead, it's one more indication that we are alone in a meaningless, futile universe.

And if Jesus is dead, then most likely we too will be dead—always dead. We may hope that God will not forget us—that somehow we will live—but we will have lost our most enticing example for thinking so. If Jesus is dead, then it appears that the fate of humanity and of all living things is to perish and be as if we had never existed at all. In such a case, the universe is absurd.

Despite these implications, many seek to be faithful to Jesus without believing God actually re-created him. It is possible to choose to trust in God and follow Jesus even if one thinks the risen Jesus is only a metaphor. It is possible to believe in the mission and healing power of the Christian community even if Jesus is not present. It is possible to have hope that God's love never lets us go even if Jesus is only dust.

But this is not the Christian faith, nor should it be. The Christian faith is that God is ultimately sovereign over all reality—including death—and that God loves us and is saving us from ourselves. This God has come to us through Jesus, has begun the future re-creation in Jesus, and given us genuine—not deluded—hope.

If God has actually re-created Jesus, then the followers of Jesus need not fear any violence, any setback, any evil, or any threat of death, because God has already conquered these in the real human drama. This is the faith by which the Christian community thrives and grows. The central nerve of the church is the proclamation that Jesus lives, that God has vindicated Jesus, that God's power flows through Jesus into us, that God's kingdom is emerging in this world, that evil has been undermined, and that God has broken the power of death.

I do not think the Christian community of faith can thrive without the conviction that Jesus actually lives. But this does not mean that the church needs to hold to a particular understanding of what exactly happened on Easter morning. We do not know what a video camera would have recorded. We do not have to have a particular understanding of what did or did not happen to his body. Does God need a corpse in order to re-create a person? Is personhood dependent on particular atoms, cells, and DNA strands? How God re-created Jesus is not available for us to know.

Even the Gospels refrain from describing the actual resurrection of Jesus. No one saw it, and the Gospel writers refused to imagine it. "Resurrection" was the best available word for Paul and the Gospel writers to use to describe what they were experiencing, but maybe even this concept is inadequate. When we talk about the resurrection of Jesus we are talking about something utterly surprising emerging into our reality—God's new act. How we can comprehend it?

In the resurrection of Jesus, faith and doubt merge in a fully appropriate way. The Gospel of Matthew says that when the disciples met the risen Jesus they worshiped him, "but some doubted." Surprisingly, these disciples are neither criticized nor excluded for their doubts; rather, they are included among those commissioned by the risen Jesus. Their doubts are not about an inability to trust and follow; their doubts are an inability to comprehend a new reality that is breaking down the doors of the previously accepted reality. That kind of doubt is not a deficit; it is the honesty and humility necessary to engage in a quest for a new understanding. The doubters are invaluable members in every congregation. They often follow Jesus more faithfully than those who loudly proclaim to believe everything in the Bible. For our faith to be genuine it must be our own, and so doubt is the hammer that constructs our own faith.

The Gospel of Mark concludes in a very strange way: a group of women run from the empty tomb, terrified by an angel's message that Jesus is risen. The Gospel ends without the risen Jesus ever being described or seen. This strikes me as a wise decision by Mark. How can one describe that which goes beyond our futile reality and fits none of our categories? How can one understand what God does? And so the risen Jesus is essentially and always a mystery—but a mystery that we experience as true, and a mystery in which we can put our trust.

5

The Right Hand of God

A healthy religious community holds clear core convictions. Since Jesus is central to the Christian faith, many Christians insist it is vital to have clear and correct ideas about who Jesus was, and who he is for us now. For instance, was he God visiting humanity in the disguise of a human being? Was he born half human, half divine? Was he a human being no different from the rest of us? Or was he, and is he, something else? Let's see how the New Testament attempts to answer this question.

After the experience of the resurrection, Jesus' followers gave him exalted titles, revealing what they believed was his true identity. But what do these titles actually mean?

One of the most frequent titles for Jesus in the New Testament is "Son of God." When we hear this title today we automatically picture in our minds a parent and a child. Except in the case of adoption, it is a biological relationship. A son literally is made from the stuff of his parents; he carries their DNA. Is this what the New Testament authors mean when they call Jesus the Son of God? Do they mean Jesus was made from the same stuff as God? Probably not. The New Testament uses the term "Son of God" as a way to describe Jesus' character and role, not his biological or spiritual substance.

In Hebrew (the language of the Old Testament) and Aramaic (the primary language of Jesus and his first followers), metaphors are frequently used to describe the quality of objects and people. "Son of . . ." is a way of describing a person's characteristics. For instance, two of Jesus' disciples, James and John, are called "sons of thunder." Does this mean they are biologically related to thunder, or that they are made of the same stuff as thunder, or that their father's name is Thunder? No. It is a way of describing their personalities. Apparently, James and John were loud or quick-tempered, so they were given the nickname "sons of thunder."

Similarly, Jesus says that peacemakers will be called "sons of God" (Matthew 5:9 RSV)—not because peacemakers are related to God or made from the same substance as God, but because they possess God's central characteristic of making peace. Jesus goes on to say that people should love their enemies and pray for their persecutors "so that you may be sons of your Father who is in heaven" (Matthew 5:45 RSV) because God also demonstrates unmerited love to wicked as well as good people. "Sons of your Father" means that these people are like God—they do what God does. In its broad usage, "son of God" simply means "godly."

So when the earliest followers of Jesus called Jesus "son of God," they were not necessarily implying that Jesus was divinely related to God; they may have been using a metaphor to describe Jesus. They were saying that Jesus is "like God"—he has characteristics in common with God's character.

Most of the time in the Bible, "son of God" is used with a more particular, special meaning. In the Old Testament, "son of God" is often used as a title for the king of Israel. Again, the king was not thought of as divinely related to God; rather, the king of Israel represented God by carrying out God's will among the people of Israel. The king was chosen by God for the holy task of upholding God's law, doing justice, and protecting the poor and the vulnerable. So when the New Testament calls Jesus the "son of God," it may be referring to Jesus as God's unique representative who exercises God's kingly authority and carries out God's will.

When used this way, "son of God" is quite similar in meaning to *messiah*, a Hebrew word that literally means "anointed one" and refers to the king of Israel. "Messiah" translated into Greek is *christos*, or "Christ," which is another extremely common way for the New Testament to refer to Jesus. So three frequent titles for Jesus—son of God, Messiah, and Christ—essentially mean the same thing. They are all referring to Jesus' kingship, representing God on earth.

At the beginning of his letter to the Christians in Rome, Paul refers to Jesus as one "who was descended from David according to the flesh and was declared to be Son of God with power according to the spirit of holiness by resurrection from the dead" (Romans 1:3–4). So for Paul, Jesus officially became "the Son of God" through his resurrection. Prior to his resurrection he was not yet, as it were, crowned by God. He was of royal descent and destined to be king, but he was not yet invested with the power of being king. The resurrection becomes Jesus' coronation; he is now invested with the authority of being God's official representative. He is now the ultimate king: the final and eternal king of Israel and, indeed, of all the world. After his resurrection, he is the Son of God (the capital "S" signifies the uniqueness of his status).

The Gospel of Mark, written about fifteen years after Paul's letter, places Jesus' status as "Son of God" at the start of his ministry rather than at his resurrection. Mark's Gospel begins with Jesus coming to be baptized by John the Baptist. The good news about Jesus begins at this point, because as Jesus comes out of the water he sees the Spirit of God come down on him like a dove, and he hears a voice from heaven say, "You are my Son, the Beloved; with you I am well pleased" (Mark 1:11).

This divine message is a combination of two statements from the Old Testament. The first comes from Psalm 2:7, in which God completes the coronation of the king of Israel by calling him "my son." The second is from Isaiah 42:1, in which God chooses a servant who is given God's Spirit for the purpose of bringing justice to the earth through gentle perseverance. In later passages in Isaiah, this servant will suffer in order to bring healing to others. By bringing these two passages together at Jesus' baptism, Jesus is being described as one who brings together two roles in the Old Testament: God's chosen king of Israel, and God's chosen servant who brings wholeness and justice through nonviolent self-giving. Mark is saying that at his baptism Jesus takes on this unique God-given identity, and so he begins his ministry.

Mark pictures Jesus' identity as the Son of God as a secret during his ministry. When the demons try to reveal his God-given identity, Jesus silences them. Jesus' disciples must figure it out on their own, but the disciples are depicted as spiritually dim-witted. When Peter finally calls Jesus "the Messiah" it seems as if the disciples have finally figured it out. But when Jesus then tells them that he must suffer and die, Peter rejects this part of Jesus' identity. The disciples are filled with visions of exercising coercive power over others, and this is the kind of king they expect Jesus to be. Jesus continually tries to correct them: the way to conquering the world is through self-giving and death. He tells them he has come, not to be served, but to serve, and to die in order to rescue others. Not until he dies on the cross does someone actually call him "God's Son"—and ironically it is the Roman soldier who crucified him. It is his crucifixion that finally reveals to others the nature of his true identity.

So, for Mark "Son of God" probably does not mean someone divinely related to God or made of the same stuff as God. "Son of God" is a unique role; it means being a king, chosen and filled with God's Spirit, who saves humanity through self-giving service.

Matthew and Luke also understand "Son of God" this way, although they push back the revealing of Jesus' God-given identity not to his baptism and crucifixion, but to his conception and birth. It is revealed to Mary, Joseph, wise men, and shepherds that this child has a special destiny to fulfill: he will become the king of the Jews and savior of the world. Again, this is a *role* that is being revealed, not a divine biological relationship or substance.

Matthew and Luke tell us that the power of the Holy Spirit caused Mary, a virgin, to conceive and give birth to Jesus. Many people mistakenly assume this means that Mary was impregnated by the Holy Spirit, so that Jesus was, in effect, made from divine stuff. This would make the Gospel stories similar to Greek myths in which Zeus or Apollo impregnate mortal women who then give birth to semi-divine heroes. But this is a serious misunderstanding of Matthew and Luke's stories. They are not telling Greek myths; that is not how they think.

God (or the Holy Spirit) is not a male with divine semen. God does not mate with or impregnate anyone. The power of the Holy Spirit refers to God's creative power. When the story says that the power of the Holy Spirit overshadowed Mary, it means that God's creative power is at work in her. The child that is conceived is not understood to be divine or semi-divine; rather, the child has a special God-given mission to fulfill.

In the Bible, various women are depicted as incapable of conceiving, and then God acts so that these women give birth. This is how God brings about the births of Isaac, Samson, Samuel, John the Baptist, and others in the Bible. These children are all seen as specially chosen by God for a particular task. Mary belongs in this group of biblical women who are able to conceive because of the power of God. What makes Mary different from the other women is that rather than being too old, she is too young—she is still a virgin! That makes her child's birth certainly more miraculous, but in the logic of biblical thinking that does not make her child more divine. Rather, Jesus' totally unique conception points to his totally unique God-given role and identity.

The other most frequent and important title for Jesus in the New Testament is "Lord." The word has at least three possible meanings in the New

Testament, and it is not always easy figuring out which sense is meant when it appears in a passage.

The most generic meaning of the word "lord" is master. It refers to anyone who exercises authority, and it is frequently used as a polite, deferential title for those who are important. To address a person as "my lord" is to acknowledge that the person has some sort of authority over the speaker. Whenever the word is used in this generic sense English translations use the lowercase "l." Jesus is sometimes called "lord" in Gospel stories by those who wish to show him respect.

"Lord" is also a name for God. In the Old Testament, Moses asks God for God's name. God replies, "I am who I am." For the ancient Israelites "I Am" was God's most sacred, intimate name (spelled "YHWH" in Hebrew). But by the time of Jesus the name of God was considered too sacred to be spoken aloud, so instead the word "Lord" replaced the divine name since God is the master of everything. (This is still true for most English translations of the Old Testament. Whenever "YHWH" appears in the original Hebrew, it is replaced by "LORD"—all capitals.)

The authors of the New Testament continued the convention of calling God "Lord." So when the New Testament also calls Jesus "Lord" it might be declaring that Jesus is God. This is what most Christians assume. But I think there is another possibility.

The third meaning of the title "Lord" is one who exercises God's authority on God's behalf. In this case, "Jesus is Lord" does not mean "Jesus is God." Rather, "Jesus is Lord" means that God has invested Jesus with all of God's power and authority. This is probably the intended meaning at the end of Peter's Pentecost speech in the second chapter of Acts. He concludes by telling the crowds, "Therefore let the entire house of Israel know with certainty that God has made him both Lord and Messiah, this Jesus whom you crucified" (Acts 2:36). If "Lord" means "God," then Peter would be saying that God has made Jesus into God. This is unlikely. What Peter is saying is that by raising Jesus from the dead God has invested Jesus with a status he did not have before: he is now the Messiah—the hoped-for king and savior of Israel; and he is Lord—he possesses all of God's authority.

Paul also makes a distinction between "God" and "Lord" when referring to Jesus. In his first letter to the Christians in Corinth he says that "there is one God, the Father, from whom are all things and for whom we exist, and one Lord, Jesus Christ, through whom are all things and through whom we exist" (1 Corinthians 8:6). Although the Lord Jesus Christ is intimately related to God, he is not the same as God; he is a conduit for God.

This understanding of the risen Jesus' relationship to God is supported by the New Testament's frequent claim that Jesus is now "at the right hand of God." In the ancient Near East the one who stood at the right hand of the king was the prime minister, who was authorized to carry out the king's will throughout the kingdom. Wherever the prime minister went, whatever the prime minister directed people to do, he was representing the king and had the king's own power. So when those earliest Christians saw Jesus after his resurrection at the right hand of God, they were claiming that Jesus is now God's immortal Prime Minister, fully representing God's authority and will.

When the earliest Christians said "Jesus is Lord" they were also making a political statement, because someone else was also claiming to be Lord: the Roman emperor. "Caesar is Lord" was stamped on much of the imperial coinage. The message was clear: give your highest loyalty to the emperor and obey him, because he has been invested with all power and authority by the gods. Those who followed Jesus made a counterclaim: Jesus, not Caesar, is Lord; he is the one who represents the true power and authority of God. As a result, early Christians refused to offer sacrifices on altars dedicated to Caesar. No wonder Christians were accused of sedition and sometimes executed when they did not renounce their faithfulness to Jesus.

In his first letter to the Christians in Corinth, Paul refers to Jesus as "the last Adam" (15:45). This term is pregnant with meaning. The first Adam, who sinned by wanting to be his own god, represents all of humanity. We are all like that first Adam (*adam* is Hebrew for "humanity"). But Jesus was a second Adam—a second chance at representing humanity. Instead of wanting to be his own god, he was fully faithful to God. He was, in a sense, the first complete human being: the first human being to have the kind of relationship with God that God always intended for all of humanity.

In his letter to the Christians in Philippi, Paul elaborates this idea: Jesus, "though he was in the form of God, did not regard equality with God as something to be exploited." Jesus did not try to grasp at God and be equal with God. Instead he "emptied himself, taking the form of a slave." Instead of committing the sin of pride, "he humbled himself and became obedient to the point of death—even death on a cross." "Therefore," Paul concludes, "God also highly exalted him and gave him the name that is above every name, so that . . . every tongue should confess that Jesus Christ is Lord" (Philippians 2:6–11).

This is a profound insight into the meaning of who Jesus is. According to Paul, Jesus has been exalted to the status of Lord because he wasn't trying to be God. Instead, Jesus was the faithful human being, emptying himself and obeying God all the way to death. Paradoxically, by emptying himself he was also fulfilling the true meaning of what it means to be God. Self-emptying love is God's central characteristic. By choosing this, Jesus was both fulfilling the proper role of humanity and embodying the deepest aspect of God.

Because of his complete humanness, because of his humble faithfulness, and because of his fulfillment of God's true nature, God raised him from the dead, investing him with God's divine authority so that heaven and earth bow to him and rightly call him "Lord." Jesus is the faithful human being who, through his death and resurrection, has now become the immortal bearer of God's nature and divine authority.

But how could Jesus of Nazareth, a human being like the rest of us, not succumb to the same pride and brokenness that all of humanity has fallen into? How did he manage to be completely faithful to God? Matthew, Mark, and Luke say that Jesus was fully infused with God's own Spirit. For Mark this infusion perhaps began at his baptism; for Matthew and Luke this infusion began with his very conception. Jesus represents a unique integration of God's Spirit and the human spirit.

That which was embodied in Jesus was from God and had always been with God. The author of Colossians says that God's Son "is the image of the invisible God, the first born of all creation," and that in him "all things in heaven and on earth were created. . . . He himself is before all things, and in him all things hold together. . . . For in him all the fullness of God was pleased to dwell, and through him God was pleased to reconcile to himself all things" (Colossians 1:16–17, 19–20). This language finds a strong echo in the beginning of John's Gospel, in which we are told that "In the beginning was the Word, and the Word was with God, and the Word was God," and that "All things came into being through him." The Word then "became flesh" (John 1:1, 3, 14)

This language for what was embodied in Jesus is very similar to language used in the Old Testament to talk about wisdom. In Proverbs 8 wisdom is personified as a female being. God creates her at the beginning of God's work. As God then goes on to create everything else, wisdom is there alongside, participating. This, of course, is metaphorical language. The Book of Proverbs is not suggesting that there is a second deity—Lady

Wisdom—who helped God create the universe. Rather, wisdom is being lifted up as being the basis of the universe. It was all made through God's wisdom. Similarly, Colossians is suggesting that God's self-giving love (fully embodied in Jesus and seen in his crucifixion) is the basis of the universe; it's been woven into the very fabric of the cosmos. For the author of Colossians, what Jesus represents is timeless, and always has been. Yes, Jesus was born and then crucified at a particular point in human history, as God's central act of rescuing humanity, but in another sense he was crucified at the foundations of the world. What Jesus represents always was and will be.

Similarly, the Gospel of John is suggesting that even though Jesus was a human being born at a particular time, he is also the full embodiment of God's timeless self-expression that brought the whole universe into being. Throughout the Gospel of John, Jesus makes exalted statements about himself, such as "before Abraham was, I am," and "I and the Father are one." After Jesus' resurrection, when Thomas declares to Jesus, "My Lord and my God," we come as close as anywhere in the New Testament to Jesus being equated with God (John 8:58; 10:30; 20:28, RSV). But as noted previously, the Gospel of John is presenting us with a spiritual interpretation of Jesus, seen in the timeless light of the resurrection; this is not how the earthly Jesus likely spoke about himself.

The Synoptic Gospels assume that Jesus, during his ministry, was not God. For instance, Mark tells us that on one occasion, when a man addressed Jesus as "Good Teacher," Jesus retorted, "Why do you call me good? No one is good but God alone" (10:17, 18). This does not mean Mark is denying Jesus' full faithfulness to God, but he is denying that Jesus, during his ministry, could be equated with God. Mark says that when Jesus was awaiting arrest he prayed to God to "remove this cup from me; yet, not what I want, but what you want" (14:36). Jesus is being presented as having his own will and desires that are different from God's, and his challenge is to submit to God's will. For Mark there is no embarrassment in distinguishing Jesus from God.

Was Jesus, during his ministry, God? I think the general consensus of the New Testament would be "no." Was Jesus, during his earthly ministry, and now after his resurrection, fully representing and embodying God's eternal character, nature, authority, and presence? The New Testament consensus is "yes." Is Jesus now immortal, sharing a divine oneness with God? Again, the consensus of the New Testament is "yes."

Jesus, in his earthly ministry, is the human metaphor for God. This gives Jesus a truly unique status in the Bible. No one else in the Bible is ever viewed as being a full reflection of God. Even Moses, the greatest figure in the Old Testament, is never viewed this way. Moses is a model of bearing God's instruction and authority, but he is not the model for the nature of God. For the Christian community, Jesus continues to be the clearest and most profound way to picture God, to understand what God is like.

I have attempted to impose some consistency and order on a subject that is not presented in a consistent and orderly fashion in the New Testament. The Gospels and letters of the New Testament contains a great variety of images and understandings of who Jesus is and was. The authors of the New Testament do not spell it all out in systematic and logical detail. They experienced God through Jesus. They spoke more in poetry and metaphor than in the analytical words of philosophy. What they knew is that in some wondrous way Jesus, in his own person and ministry, uniquely and fully reveals God for us. There is a oneness between God and Jesus Christ, and the continuing presence and power of God's Spirit.

As the first few centuries went by, the church attempted to explain the exact nature of Jesus Christ, and his relationship to God and the Holy Spirit, using the categories of Greek philosophy. The result was the intricate and carefully balanced doctrine of the Trinity, in which the Father, Son, and Holy Spirit are said to be of the same "substance"—one God—but are separate "persons." This has led to the charge that Christians believe in three gods instead of one God, though Christians have strenuously objected to this characterization. The doctrine of the Trinity is an important and fruitful doctrine for the church; for one thing, it suggests that relational love is at the heart of God. But it suffers from the limitations of being an artificial construct based on Greek philosophy. The Bible is not Greek philosophy, and the doctrine of the Trinity cannot do full justice to the more dynamic, metaphorical, and multifaceted experiences and expressions in the New Testament.

In the end, it is not the language and titles and philosophical conclusions about Jesus that matter the most to the Christian faith. Intellectual beliefs in certain doctrines are not as important as faithfulness to God, and faithfulness to Jesus Christ, who shows us God. The clear core convictions that give the Christian faith its greatest vitality and health are not about defining Jesus' divine identity but about making Jesus *our* Lord. It is unfortunate that what we *think* about Jesus has often replaced *following* Jesus as the true test of faith.

One of the advantages of understanding Jesus through the New Testament rather than through later creeds is that we potentially open up more common ground with the Jewish and Muslim communities. Certainly the New Testament understands Jesus in ways quite distinctive from these other faith communities, and we should not diminish the New Testament witness and experience. But if we can hold our philosophical and creedal statements more humbly, we can more fruitfully advance our dialogue and common mission, and we will then be able to bring more healing to the world.

I am encouraged that recently within Judaism, despite centuries of persecution by those who called themselves Christians, there is a growing appreciation for Jesus. The popular theologian Rabbi Harold Kushner has said, "[Jesus is] the instrument through which my God, the God of the Hebrew Bible, becomes the universal God. . . . [T]hrough the story of the passion, the crucifixion, and the resurrection he comes to embody the idea of a God . . . who suffers, a God who shares with us our human vulnerability and triumphs over vulnerability."[1]

To understand Jesus' meaning for today we need to explore one more aspect of his ministry: his crucifixion. At the heart of Jesus' significance is not only his resurrection, but also his suffering and death. Indeed, the central symbol of the Christian faith is a cross, not an empty tomb. Consider how odd that is. The cross was a gruesome instrument of torture and execution used by the Romans for criminals, and yet Christians place a cross at the front of their places of worship, and sometimes wear small crosses around their necks. It would be similar to hanging a needle around one's neck, or placing an electric chair in the front of the sanctuary. Why did the most brutal and humiliating form of state execution become the symbol of the Christian faith? Because it reveals the most crucial truths about humanity and God.

The cross reveals the depth of human distortion. Human beings are so blind, so fearful, so grasping for their own power that they would even crucify a person who reflects God. There is a Jewish saying, "If God lived on earth, people would throw stones through his windows." The cross reveals the same truth, except in more brutal detail. During the American

---

1. Author's transcription from a video from the 1990s featuring Harold Kushner and other religious leaders and scholars responding to the question, "Who is Jesus?"

civil rights movement, African-Americans who peacefully demonstrated for a place to sit at the lunch counter, or on the bus, or in the school were sometimes beaten, hosed down, bitten by dogs, arrested, or even murdered. When these images were televised, they shocked the nation into a realization of just how racist and violent American society actually was. Similarly, the cross shocks us into a realization of just how blind and brutal we are.

Some years ago a man in Paraguay spoke out against the injustices of the government. The police, in retaliation, arrested his son and tortured him to death. Rather than dressing his son and covering his wounds for the funeral, the father decided to put his dead son on display exactly as he had found him—naked, burned, beaten, and lying on a blood-soaked mattress. As the townspeople passed by the boy's tortured body at the funeral, it was the most devastating protest of all, revealing the truth about the government.[2] The cross is also a funeral that puts our own evil and injustice on display.

The most disturbing irony of Jesus' crucifixion is that he was executed not by the most despicable people and institutions of his time, but by some of the best. They thought what they were doing was right. Some religious leaders believed that Jesus was misrepresenting God's laws and was a danger to true faith; the chief priests were concerned about preventing a riot in the temple during Passover; the Roman government saw itself as providing the gift of law and order. In this sense, Jesus' execution is similar to that of Socrates', in which the first democracy in the world—the epitome of enlightened politics—voted to have its wisest citizen killed. So the cross shows us that even at our best we are still blind; even when we think we are doing right we are prone to do wrong. We are not capable of fixing our own evil, straightening out our own distortion. Our brokenness is always there. The cross hints at how hopeless human nature really is.

The cross reveals God suffering with us. Human life is often filled with suffering. Tragedies occur, loved ones die, illnesses rack our bodies, and brutalities are committed against the innocent. In such a world we feel abandoned. Life is meaningless and absurd. God is nowhere.

Elie Wiesel, the Jewish philosopher who, as a boy, was a prisoner in a Nazi concentration camp, tells the story of another boy who, along with two men, was caught taking part in a plot. Their punishment was public hanging. Everyone in the concentration camp was forced to watch as the chairs were kicked away. Then everyone had to file past and see the offenders swinging from their ropes, suffocating. Hardest of all was watching the boy—who had

2. Yancey, *Disappointment with God*, 185–86.

the face of a sad angel—slowly choking to death for over half an hour. Wiesel heard a man behind him ask, "Where is God now?" Wiesel looked at the hanging boy and thought, "He is hanging here on the gallows."[3]

Wiesel was not suggesting that this was comforting. On the contrary, his point was that God died in that concentration camp. The cross of Jesus, in a way, agrees. Jesus represents the presence of God, not only in his life, but also in his death. So when Jesus dies, God, in a sense, also dies. But because of the resurrection, this gruesome scene becomes a source of comfort. The cross shows us that God shares our humanity, our suffering, all the way to death. God is not aloof, dispassionate; God has gone with us into the depths of suffering.

The cross reveals the depth of God's love which can break through our self-centeredness. During World War II a group of British soldiers and officers captured by the Japanese were forced to build a bridge in the jungle over the River Kwai. Because of the brutal conditions under which they worked, resentments ran deep and tempers easily flared. One day, during a tool count, it was discovered that one of the shovels was missing. A Japanese guard lined up the prisoners and began screaming at them. He waved a cocked rifle in their faces and said he would kill all of them if the one who stole the shovel did not step forward. One of the prisoners stepped forward and said, "I did it." The guard beat him to death. At the next tool count, it was discovered that all the shovels were accounted for—no shovel had been stolen after all. The man who had been beaten to death was innocent and had stepped forward to save the lives of the others. His act of self-sacrifice had a profound effect on the prisoners, changing their attitudes toward each other and toward their captors.[4]

Since Jesus represents God's nature and presence, his death represents God's self-giving love, going all the way to the cross for us. The apostle Paul is astonished when he contemplates the depth of God's love. He says in his letter to the Christians in Rome, "Indeed, rarely will anyone die for a righteous person—though perhaps for a good person someone might actually dare to die. But God proves his love for us in that while we were still sinners Christ died for us" (5:7–8). It's noble when someone is willing to die for a close friend, but it's astonishing when someone dies for those who hate him. Jesus died, not for the best people, but for all people—even those who crucified him. While being nailed to the cross he said, "Father,

---

3. Wiesel, *Night*, 60–62.

4. Gordon, *To End All Wars*, 101–2.

forgive them, for they do not know what they are doing" (Luke 23:34). This is the depth of God's love. It has no prior conditions, and it is not limited to certain people. Whether we love God, ignore God, hate God, or crucify God makes no difference to the love of God—it is poured out even to death.

This act of self-giving love is so profound it has the power to break through the self-centeredness and fear that are at the root of human nature and are the cause of our misery. By looking at the cross of Christ we are empowered to love as God loves. As one author of the Bible says, "We love because he first loved us" (1 John 4:19). We do not know how to love until it is shown to us. Through the cross, God has given us the ultimate example and inspiration.

The cross reveals the power by which evil is defeated in the universe. In the Book of Revelation, the author has a vision in which he sees what is going on in heaven. He sees God sitting on a throne, and in God's right hand is a scroll in which is written the completion and healing of the universe. But the scroll is sealed, and so an angel proclaims, "Who is worthy to open the scroll and break the seals?" No one is found in heaven or earth who is strong enough and worthy enough to open the scroll and bring creation and the human drama to its rightful conclusion. Then, just when it looks like no one can be found, it is announced that "the Lion of the tribe of Judah, the Root of David, has conquered, so that he can open the scroll and its seven seals." But who steps forward to take the scroll from God's hand? A lamb that has been slaughtered (Revelation 5).

Individual evil, institutional evil, and cosmic evil—everything that is in rebellion against God—has been defeated not by force or strength or armies, but by self-sacrificing love at the cross. The power of evil is overcome, not by killing it, but by absorbing it with the opposite. The constant refrain throughout the vision in Revelation is that the Lamb has conquered—not "will conquer" but "has conquered." The Lamb has already defeated cosmic evil at the cross, and so the end of evil is already certain, and the healing of creation is guaranteed. How do we know the cross defeated evil? Because of the resurrection. The resurrection is God's vindication that the way of the cross, the way of self-giving love, ultimately triumphs.

Paul places this revolutionary message about the nature of God's power at the heart of his good news. "For the message about the cross is foolishness to those who are perishing, but to us who are being saved it is the power of God." The cross represents the opposite of the world's definition of power. God's power is gentle, kind, constant, persuasive, and self-giving. It does not retaliate, hate, or use the weapons of violence. "For God's foolishness is wiser than human wisdom, and God's weakness is stronger than human strength" (1 Corinthians 1:18, 25).

The cross reveals a way to follow. This is not only how God defeats evil; it is also how God wants us to defeat evil. The cross is meant to be an example to be followed. It points to a way of life that brings wholeness. Jesus said during his ministry, "If any want to become my followers, let them deny themselves and take up their cross and follow me. For those who want to save their life will lose it, and those who lose their life for my sake, and for the sake of the gospel [the good news], will save it" (Mark 13:34–35). This idea of self-giving resulting in our own rescue is expressed well in the so-called "Prayer of Saint Francis," which concludes with the words, "For it is in giving that we receive, it is in pardoning that we are pardoned, and it is in dying that we are born to eternal life."

Throughout his ministry Jesus stood for nonviolence and reconciliation. He taught that we should respond to abuse with prayers, to lawsuits with positive action, to theft with generosity. The cross is an extension of this teaching. Paul echoes Jesus' teachings when he gives ethical guidance to the Christians in Rome. Quoting first from Proverbs, he says, "No, 'if your enemies are hungry, feed them; if they are thirsty, give them something to drink; for by doing this you will heap burning coals [of remorse] on their heads.' Do not be overcome by evil, but overcome evil with good" (Romans 12:20–21). The way of the cross is not simply a final act of self-sacrifice; it is an entire way of life of responding to others, regardless of circumstances, with love.

Early Christians did not just reverence Jesus; they imitated him. The cross was not just a cosmic drama for Jesus alone to enact, but an example to be followed by all. First Peter 2:21 summarizes this well when it says, "For to this you have been called, because Christ also suffered for you, leaving you an example, so that you should follow in his steps."

The cross reveals a sacrifice for the forgiveness of our sins. Religion in the ancient world almost always revolved around animal sacrifice. One demonstrated loyalty, gratitude, or remorse to God (or the gods) by offering a sacrifice on an altar. In return, heaven offered good fortune for one's crops or family, or forgiveness for one's sin. The blood of an animal, sprinkled on the altar, washed away one's guilt. It is hard for our culture, which does not practice animal sacrifice, to appreciate the power and meaningfulness of this ritual system. But if we put ourselves in the place of those early followers of Jesus, we can begin to glimpse the wonder with which they apprehended Jesus' sacrifice.

The earliest Christians turned to their Bible—the Old Testament—to make sense of Jesus' shocking crucifixion. There they found the Exodus story of Hebrew slaves putting blood from lambs on the doorposts of their homes so that the angel of death would pass over them, resulting in their freedom from Egyptian slavery. In the Book of Isaiah they found a description of a servant who would take the sins of others on himself, bearing their punishment, bringing healing to all. In these passages the early Christians saw Jesus, and they had a tremendous realization: Jesus has become our Passover Lamb who frees us from slavery! Jesus is the servant who bears the sins of the world!

We human beings are sinful. Despite our remorse, despite our attempts to do good, and despite our animal sacrifices we continue to stray from God's will and fall back into sin. Everything we touch we distort with our own selfishness and immaturity. We cannot reach God and we cannot make ourselves right with God. So God does for us what we cannot do for ourselves. Because Jesus was completely faithful to God and innocent, his death on the cross represented the greatest religious sacrifice that could ever take place. It was a sacrifice that covered not just some sins for some people for some of the time, but all the sins of the entire world for all time. By committing ourselves to God and the way of Jesus, we take on the merits of his sacrifice. His faithfulness becomes our faithfulness. His innocence becomes our innocence. Through the sacrifice on the cross God has reconciled the world to God's self; we have only to accept it with gratitude.

This view of the cross has been extremely powerful and meaningful for millions of Christians; it has also been puzzling and problematic. For instance, is this view suggesting God is incapable of forgiving us without Jesus being tortured and killed? Even we flawed human beings are capable of forgiving others without requiring a human sacrifice. Surely God's ability to forgive is greater than ours. But this problem is eliminated if we see the cross not as an act that *enables* God's forgiveness, but that *reveals* God's forgiveness. The cross is a sign of God's timeless forgiveness—supplying what we cannot supply, saving us from ourselves. God does what we cannot. God makes the sacrifice that we cannot. God covers our sins—we do not.

Is Jesus the Son of God—embodying God's Spirit, representing God's nature, enacting God's saving love? That is a truth we either experience or do not experience. After we contemplate the person we meet in the Gospel stories, and celebrate with the community of faith that embodies his continuing presence, we come to our own conclusions. For the Christian community of faith, the answer is "yes." And so we follow.

6

The Path to Wholeness

I used to volunteer at a chemical dependency center that operated in a community hospital. People addicted to alcohol or other drugs would go through a four-week residential program that included detoxification, education, individual and group therapy, and working through the first five steps of the Alcoholics Anonymous program. The first three steps of the famous twelve-step AA program use spiritual language: "1. We admitted we were powerless over alcohol—that our lives had become unmanageable. 2. Came to believe that a Power greater than ourselves could restore us to sanity. 3. Made a decision to turn our will and our lives over to the care of God as we understand Him."

A new patient was brought into the chemical dependency center and introduced to these first three steps. As an agnostic he objected to the spiritual language and argued with his counselor, "What kind of religious garbage is this? What are you forcing me to believe in?" His counselor responded, "There's only one thing you have to believe: there is a God, and you ain't it."

Perhaps all spiritual growth and healing begins with this discovery. Through it we are enabled to mature, love others as ourselves, seek help from others, nurture deep friendships, connect with the transcendent, and bring needed benefits to the world. It's also the central truth of the biblical story and the Christian faith: there is a God, and we ain't it.

From what I have gleaned so far from my readings of other religions, it appears to me that every religion—Buddhism, Hinduism, Islam, Judaism, Christianity, etc.—believes there is something seriously amiss with humanity, and one of the purposes of religion is to help solve that problem. Human beings do not live unreflective lives as the rest of the animal kingdom seems to do; rather, we are conscious that there is something often "out of whack" with us. What is the problem? The human race has lots of problems: guilt, alienation, anxiety, broken relationships, resentments, perpetual violence, social oppression, extreme poverty, environmental degradation, fear of death, etc. One of the factors that makes religion a universal phenomenon, capable of affecting us in the most profound ways, is that it looks deeply into the human dilemma and seeks to answer our most fundamental needs.

Each religion understands the cause of the human dilemma somewhat differently, and the beliefs and practices of that religion flow out of the way it attempts to solve that dilemma. Christianity, Judaism, and Islam share a common understanding of the essential cause of the human dilemma: we human beings are in a broken relationship with the true God of all reality. Why is that relationship broken? Because we are not God-centered. Instead, we are fear-centered—jerked around by our anxieties and insecurities; and we are self-centered—pursuing our own interests and desires first. The result of this ruptured relationship with God is that we are also in a ruptured relationship with others, nature, and even with ourselves. Our attitudes and actions do harm to the wholeness of others, to the health of the environment, and to our own genuine fulfillment. On an international scale, governments are locked in a greedy competition for resources, wealth, and domination. Life is a power game of getting what one wants and creating elaborate excuses and myths to make it all look justified and glorious. And hanging over it all is the desperation of facing death, possible oblivion, and utter meaninglessness.

The Christian faith is about getting us out of this anxious, self-destructive pattern and restoring us to God-centeredness.

How do we become God-centered? If it were easy, and the benefits obvious, humanity would frequently be God-centered. Instead, we have an addiction to fear and selfishness that keeps pulling us away from putting our lives in God's hands. Somehow this addiction must be overcome. Like a chemical addiction, it cannot be removed—we always have it. But there is a way to become a recovering addict: a person with an addiction who maintains sobriety and puts a decent life together again.

In AA the first step is to learn that one is addicted. Addiction, by definition, means one has a diminished capacity to control a certain compulsive behavior that is causing harm to one's life. If we could control our destructive habits through willpower, we would (or at least we would once the costs became greater than the benefits). The fact that we continue destructive habits, even when they ruin our relationships and happiness, makes it obvious we are addicted.

But we human beings are loathe to admit that we have destructive attitudes and behaviors that we can't handle ourselves. Our addiction to self-centeredness blinds us to the fact that we are addicted to self-centeredness. Instead we try to heal all of the world's problems, and our own, with our own willpower and self-centeredness in place. American culture, in general, is based on the premise that with enough ingenuity, education, opportunity, and hard work we can solve all our problems. Whatever messes we have gotten into, science or the military or our favorite political party can get us out of. Our money says "In God We Trust"—which is true, because money is our god. If we have enough of it, we think, the problems of the world can be solved.

I do not mean to suggest that we human beings, even in our selfishness and fear, are incapable of doing wonders. On the contrary, human achievements in art, science, philosophy, and social organization are stunning. I enjoy and appreciate the creations of humanity. But if we want wholeness, if we want peace within and peace without, then we must take the next step and say to ourselves, "There is a God, and I ain't it."

What is God? Alcoholics Anonymous, as a non-sectarian organization, makes a point of not defining God, other than as "a Power greater than ourselves." As a result, members of AA imagine God in all sorts of ways: as a supreme personal being, an impersonal force, the AA support group, or something else. But what's crucial is that God is that which is greater than ourselves. No concept of God is of any spiritual usefulness if it does not begin with the realization that God is greater than ourselves; otherwise we are God, and we are right back to our initial dilemma of self-centeredness.

According to the Christian faith, for God to bring wholeness to the entire human situation, not just to individuals, God needs to be greater than the willpower and abilities of humanity as a whole. The human dilemma is not solved by us as individuals, nor by all of us working together (though working together has great advantages over working alone!). God is not the "spirit of humanity"; that's simply self-centeredness writ large. Rather, God must be something beyond us—a kind of power that is beyond all human-centered power.

But if our wholeness depends on a kind of power that is beyond all human-centered power, then by definition it is a power that we cannot access ourselves and make use of as we see fit. If we can control it, then we are God. And so this power beyond all human power, if it is to bring us wholeness, must take the initiative and reach out to us. God must be gracious to us.

This is how the biblical story depicts God. God is beyond us, God is ultimate power (though a very different kind of power than self-centered power!), and God is gracious to us—reaching out to help us. In the biblical story God is continuously reaching out to humanity with acts of grace. "Grace" means favor. In other words, God favors us; God is on our side; God loves us. This grace has no preconditions; it is a gift to us all, no strings attached. God reveals this grace to us in a multitude of ways: through the ridiculous abundance of nature; through the human experience of awe, creativity, and love; and through seeing "the hand of God" at work in the human story.

The ancient Israelites, in particular, saw God's grace at work in history when they were freed from slavery in Egypt, received God's law at Mt. Sinai, and eventually moved into a land of promise. The Bible is the grace-filled story of God—despite human selfishness and fear, and despite tragedies and disillusionment—slowly working out a way to save humanity from its own self-destruction. The story, as we have seen, comes to a climax in the story of God's grace embodied, God's grace crucified, and God's grace risen again. Christians call this "the gospel," which is from an Old English word meaning "good news."

But there is still a problem: God can extend infinite grace to us, but unless we receive it—unless we believe in it and accept it—its full effect is prevented. So the good news of the Christian faith also involves our response: trust.

Trust is like learning how to swim. I had great difficulty learning how to swim when I was a boy because I wouldn't trust the water to hold me up. Whenever I gazed into that deep, dark water I became afraid, and when the water came up around my head, into my ears or nose, I panicked and sank. Many times I pretended to be swimming when in actuality I was simply flailing my arms and bouncing along on tiptoe against the bottom of the lake or pool. Then, after years of splashing in the water, I discovered one day almost by accident that I could float if I just relaxed and gave myself to the water.

When we experience God's grace deeply enough, when we splash around in it long enough, we discover that grace will hold us up if we simply trust in it. This is how God's grace finally breaks through our addiction to being fear-centered and self-centered. We trust in God's grace; we relax and we let go. Grace empowers us to turn the center of our lives over to God. This act of letting go and trusting in God fills us with the same Spirit of God that filled Jesus. Now we are no longer self-centered but God-centered, no long fear-centered but trust-centered.

Trusting in God means, essentially, trusting that love is the ultimate rule and reality of the universe. Since we have been buoyed up by love, now we can share love. Love is not selfish. By definition, it is self-giving for the benefit of others. God has enabled us to become like God, having God's central characteristic of love. We are truly a different kind of human being—"born again" as the Gospel of John puts it. Or as Paul says, "it is no longer I who live, but it is Christ who lives in me" (Galatians 2:20). Our sharing of this love is the beginning of wholeness for the world.

None of this is our achievement; it is a gift given to us by God, a gift in which we put our trust. If it were our achievement, then this would lead us back into self-centeredness, congratulating ourselves on our wonderful insight or ability to trust. Paul summarizes the good news of the Christian faith in these words: "For by grace you have been saved through faith, and this is not your own doing; it is the gift of God—not the result of works, so that no one may boast" (Ephesians 2:8–9).

Greg Louganis, who twice won gold medals in the Olympic high dive, was asked by a reporter what he did to keep his composure during his final dive in the 1984 Olympics. Louganis replied, "I was scared going into the last dive. But I stood there and told myself that no matter what I do here, my mother will still love me."[1]

The extraordinary task for Louganis was to make near-perfect dives. How did he do it? One essential factor was trusting in his mother's love. His mother extended grace to him, loving him whether he succeeded or failed. This grace empowered him, allowed him to relax, enabling him to make perfect dives. But for that grace to empower him he had to believe in it. He had to have faith in his mother's unconditional love. As Paul might say it: Greg was "saved" by his mother's grace through his faith. Similarly, our trust in God's grace empowers us.

In the original language of the New Testament, the words for "believe," "faith," and "trust" are all the same word. In English, though, they can have very different connotations. "Believe" often refers to a cognitive activity, as in, "I believe the world is round." "Faith" often refers to a body of beliefs, as

---

1. Mifflin, "Portrait of Power and Grace."

in "the Christian faith." "Trust," on the other hand, always has the sense of relying on someone or something; there is always the element of surrender, letting go, not worrying. This is what the New Testament means when it talks about how we should relate to God. To believe in God does not mean, primarily, that one believes God exists. Faith in Jesus does not mean, primarily, giving assent to the doctrine that he is the Son of God. To believe in God, or to have faith in Jesus, means to trust—to let go and hand over one's life to that which grounds all of reality in self-giving love.

Unlike learning how to swim, in which once you've learned to trust the water you never forget, trust in God is easily forgotten. It does not continue automatically; it has to be nurtured and renewed on a continual basis. Just as many recovering alcoholics, in order to maintain sobriety, need to continually go through the twelve-step program and regularly receive support from an AA group, so we, in order to maintain God-centeredness, need to continually turn over ourselves to God and receive the support of a faith community. Just as a recovering alcoholic is still an alcoholic, so we, even as we are God-centered, still tend toward self-centeredness.

The fact is we never turn our entire lives over to God, at least not for long. We may say we do, and we may sincerely want to, but there are always hidden parts of us that are seeking control. Deep under the water, hidden from view, a toe is touching the bottom of the lake from time to time. Even the most committed members of the faith community are a mixture of God-centeredness, fear-centeredness, and self-centeredness. It is so much easier for us to trust in ourselves than to trust in God that we inevitably mix them together. Jesus frequently admonished his disciples for having "little faith." The problem was not that they were without trust in God; the problem was that their fears were greater. When Paul says, "It is no longer I who live, but it is Christ who lives in me" (Galatians 2:20), he's talking about an ideal state, not one that he was able to maintain at all times (as can be seen in his more intemperate outbursts in his letters!).

One time a man asked Jesus to heal his son "if you are able." Jesus retorted, "If you are able!—All things can be done for the one who believes." The man then cried out, "I believe; help my unbelief!" (Mark 9:22–24). This man is a picture of all of us who wish to be followers of Jesus and trust in God. Jesus continually assures us that God can be trusted, and that all the powers of God's wholeness are available to us when we trust. So we let go—sometimes a lot, and sometimes a little, but rarely fully, and never always.

This means that our wholeness is never complete in our lifetime, and the world's wholeness is never completed during the normal course of history. We are not "saved"—completed and in the past tense; we are "being saved"—a continuous activity.

Many Christians believe that being saved means that when they die they will live forever with God. Certainly the Christian faith includes the conquering of our fear of death. We trust that God's love—a love that is willing to go all the way to the cross for us—does not abandon us at death. Paul puts it most eloquently when he writes to the Christians in Rome, "Who will separate us from the love of Christ? Will hardship, or distress, or persecution, or famine, or nakedness, or peril, or sword? . . . No, in all these things we are more than conquerors through him who loved us. For I am convinced that neither death, nor life, nor angels, nor rulers, nor things present, nor things to come, nor powers, nor height, nor depth, nor anything else in all creation, will be able to separate us from the love of God in Christ Jesus our Lord" (Romans 8:35–39).

But if being saved only refers to what happens to us after death, then that means that God has abandoned hope for this world and the human drama. That would mean that the Christian faith is essentially escapism: it has no solution for the world's problems and the human dilemma, so it waits till we die to rocket the souls of the faithful to a perfect world called heaven. This is not the biblical story and this is not the Christian faith.

What are the Ten Commandments for if they are not for guiding a new community on earth that brings wholeness? What is the Book of Proverbs for if it is not to show the path of true wisdom for living one's daily life? What are the writings of the prophets for if they are not for calling their societies back to doing God's justice and creating peace? What are the ethical teachings of Jesus for if they are not for training disciples to begin living out the kingdom of God here on earth?

The task of the faith community is not garnering souls for an afterlife in heaven. The essential task of the faith community is to live out the kingdom of God and bring God's wholeness to the world right now. Salvation is for our bodies and minds; it is for the human community; it is even for creation itself. All is to be healed. Genesis says that when God created the world, God said, "It is good." God loves nature and God loves the human drama. God desires all of it to be made whole. This is the meaning of salvation.

The Book of Isaiah contains visions of a time coming in which God's will is truly being done by all people and all nations. When that time comes, people will beat their swords into plow blades and their spears into pruning hooks. War will be a thing of the past as people live in peace with each other. Nations that were formerly attacking or being attacked, like wolves and sheep, will lie down together without violence or harm. This ideal condition will come about when the earth is filled with the knowledge of God's true goodness and grace—"as the waters cover the sea" (Isaiah 11:6–9). Is this intended to be a picture of heaven—of a disembodied life after death on another plane of existence? No. Isaiah is talking about humanity's future hope on earth. It is an ideal which we are meant to believe in and strive for.

Salvation for this world and salvation after death are actually one and the same; they become fused together in the Bible so that they cannot truly be distinguished. Fostering communities of love and healing, out of gratitude to God's grace, makes us part of God's kingdom now. After death we remain in that kingdom.

The final book of the Bible, Revelation, announces the coming of "a new heaven and a new earth," and a "new Jerusalem" coming to earth. Into that city "the kings of the earth" (governments) "bring their glory" (the creativity of human culture). Though the author uses fantastic, other-worldly images, he's still talking about earth, not heaven. In other words, the biblical hope is that God's heaven (the condition of completeness and wholeness) becomes fused with earth. As Jesus prayed, "Your kingdom come. Your will be done, on earth as it is in heaven" (Matthew 6:10).

Can we really believe that such a thing can happen? Can we truly believe that peace and wholeness will come to the earth? It certainly won't happen if we remain self-centered and fearful. If it happens, it will be God's doing. It will be "the day of the Lord" or "the coming of the Son of Humanity." One of the earliest Christian prayers was "Maranatha!"—our Lord, come! In other words, for God's wholeness to fully come into our world will require more than what we can do by all our sciences and best efforts.

But even if it is by God's doing, it is also with our faithful participation. Through trust we are partners with God in bringing wholeness to the world. According to the New Testament, our transformation has already begun: "if anyone is in Christ, there is a new creation" (2 Corinthians 5:17). As Jesus said, the reign of God is already dawning: it is like a tiny mustard seed that is now growing and defying all expectations; it is like wheat and weeds growing up together until the harvest. When humanity's growth is fully ripened then God will bring everything to its goal. We don't have to understand how it happens or what it will look like. We can leave the final outcome in God's hands. But our task is clear: live it out now.

We do this not as individuals fighting the good fight on our own, but together as a community of faith. Our strategy is to create a community of wholeness that keeps us grounded in God and becomes a witness to the larger human community. If we work individually, from within the world's self-centered systems, we will not get very far in spreading wholeness. Quite likely, we will get sucked back into fear and selfishness by these societies and governments that are so much larger than we are. But when we create a faith community that shares its possessions, meets the needs of those at hand, serves each other with joy, reconciles broken relationships, and worships God with gratefulness, we are showing the world another way of being a community together. This healing community grounds us and strengthens us when we need to engage the world's self-centered systems.

This truly is salvation: not just believing some specific doctrines, not just saying, "Jesus is my Lord and Savior," but actually enacting and experiencing the healing of human brokenness. The evidence of our wholeness in God is not the words coming out of our mouths or the beliefs in our heads; it is the God-centered life we live together. Jesus had no time for empty statements of loyalty. He didn't care if people called him "Lord" if they didn't follow his example. For him the test of genuine loyalty to God was clear: look at the fruit that is produced. The Letter of James makes the same point: true religion is helping the poor and vulnerable, and faith without doing good is dead. If wholeness is not lived out, it is not genuine trust in God.

Too often the Christian faith has been boiled down to "believing in" a certain doctrine or formula. A favorite Bible verse that many use to summarize the Christian faith is John 3:16, which says, "For God so loved the world that he gave his only Son, so that everyone who believes in him may not perish but may have eternal life." As true as this verse is, isolated by itself it can distort the Christian faith. It can easily leave the false impression that all God wants is for us is believe (with our heads) that Jesus is God's Son so we can live forever in heaven. This makes no moral sense, and the world is left unhealed. I think there may be verses that better encapsulate what the Christian faith is after.

A true story: A traveling Christian evangelist asked a man after a revival service, "Are you saved?" The man replied, "Yes." The evangelist asked him, "And what verse do you have to prove it?" The man answered, "1 John 3:14: 'We know that we have passed from death to life because we love one another.'" The evangelist, taken aback by this unexpected answer, sputtered, "Y-y-you have the wrong verse!" No, it was a better verse.

When we do the good that God desires, we must be watchful for two common pitfalls that will undermine the wholeness God is working toward. The first pitfall is doing good in order to be loved, and the second is pride.

When we love in order to be loved, it is not love that we are giving—it is a self-centered exchange with a hidden agenda. If the other doesn't return our "love" we become frustrated, perhaps even despising the other. But genuine love cares for the other regardless of that person's response. The person is loved simply because each person has intrinsic worth. So love means extending ourselves to others for their benefit, not for our own. This does not mean we do harm to ourselves in order to benefit another; rather, as Jesus says, we love our neighbor as ourselves.

Our love for God, and doing good for the sake of realizing God's reign, works the same way. If we are doing good so that God will love us, or love us more, then our motivation is self-centered. This is not love; this is not the self-giving grace God has shown us. We love because God has already loved us. We do good because God has already done so much good for us. Our response is one of joy, not need; gratitude, not guilt. Our good is not done in order to make up for our previous failures; it is not motivated by shame or a need for forgiveness. Forgiveness has already been received. We can't repay our debt, so God has already canceled it. As soon as we respond to God's grace with trust and grateful submission of our life, the relationship between God and us is restored.

We couldn't increase God's love for us even if we wanted to. It is already fully there. God's love is genuine—given to us without strings attached. Our self-esteem is not something we achieve through worthy accomplishments; it is a gift given to us as soon as we were created. All of our actions done for God are done because we want to do them. It is not a burdensome obligation to be paid off, nor is it a way to merit eternal life with God. It is all done out of grateful joy.

The Ten Commandments—the epitome of religious and moral obligations in the minds of many people—do not begin with the words, "You shall . . . ." The commandments begin with this preamble: "I am the LORD your God, who brought you out of the land of Egypt, out of the house of slavery"

(Exodus 20:2). In other words, the Ten Commandments begin with a statement of grace: "I, God, have already rescued you; now here's what I want you to do in return." In the Bible grace comes first, then comes our grateful response of discipleship. It is never the other way around.

If we love God only to get good things from God, then what happens when life brings us tragedy? Then our "love" for God turns into bitterness. The realm of nature has an element that is chaotic and unpredictable. Nature is amoral; it will not treat us fairly, and God-centered people are not given special exemptions. Will we still love God when tragedy strikes? Will we still give of ourselves for the sake of the world's wholeness? If our love for God is for God, not ourselves, then we will.

The second pitfall to doing good is pride. Jesus tells a story about two men who go to the temple to pray. One is a very religious man and the other is a tax collector who is a collaborator for an oppressive, foreign empire. The religious man thanks God that he is not a thief or an adulterer or employed as a tax collector. He tells God how dedicated he is to God through his self-sacrifices and generous giving. But when the tax collector prays he faces the floor in shame and cries out, "God, be merciful to me, a sinner." Jesus concludes the story by saying that it is the tax collector whose relationship with God was restored that day, not the religious man's (Luke 18:13–14).

This story turns upside down our usual assumptions about who deserves what. The point is: no one deserves God's grace, and no one achieves God's forgiveness and restoration. God's grace is free, and the only appropriate response to it is humble trust. God-centeredness rests on humility, not pride. We have achieved nothing; we have been given everything. The good we do is not to show off or to compare ourselves to others. If we do then we have lost our humility. When we compare ourselves to others, congratulating ourselves for being better than someone else, then we are assuming we are more deserving of God's favor, and we are undermining a loving relationship with others. Moral self-congratulation destroys the wholeness we are trying to create. Our very goodness defeats itself.

But our own goodness isn't the only thing we sometimes take pride in. Self-centeredness is so sneaky that we sometimes take pride in our "humble trust"! We congratulate ourselves that we have the good sense to put our trust in God (unlike those atheists over there!). Or we congratulate ourselves for putting our trust in the right God (unlike those Hindus over there!). This is just as destructive as congratulating ourselves on our goodness. Remember the tax collector in the story: he simply pleads for mercy.

God's grace is free, and our trust in God's grace is an act of humility and appreciation, or it is not trust in grace at all.

Trust, gratitude, and humility lead to doing God-centered good, and God-centered good helps to bring wholeness to our relationships and the world. Without wholeness in our relationships there can be no healing community. But what happens if we fail to do good? What if we slip up and do harm to others? Is the possibility of wholeness lost whenever we wrong others? No. Our failures are inevitable, and so confession and forgiveness within the community of faith are essential for maintaining our course toward wholeness.

When we wrong others, and become aware of it, we should confess to those we've offended and make amends. We cannot control their response, but our hope is that we will be offered forgiveness—a letting go of hostile feelings and a pardoning of the offense.

When someone wrongs us we should share our feelings of pain so that the situation is brought into the light for growth and possible healing. We foster an attitude of caring toward the offender, and gradually let go of bitter feelings within us. If the person admits the wrong done to us, wishing to make amends, we release the person from feeling guilt, offering our pardon.

Forgiveness is often complicated. The greater the offense and harm, the more difficult the process of forgiveness is likely to be. It is not something we can rush, nor force ourselves (or the other) to offer. It has to be the honest and free result of pain shared, mutual listening and understanding, responsibility taken, and new commitments established. It is made possible by our realization that we all need forgiveness, and we have all been offered forgiveness by God.

God's goal for humanity is that broken relationships be reconciled, among individuals as well as among ethnic groups, races, religions, and nations. Human reconciliation reflects divine reconciliation. Without reconciliation wholeness is incomplete, and the reign of God is not yet present among us.

Can every broken relationship be healed? No, not in our lifetimes. But our task is to be agents of grace, imitating the grace of God, perhaps making possible what once was impossible. As Paul says, reflecting the teaching of Jesus, "Bless those who persecute you; bless and do not curse them. . . . If it is possible, so far as it depends on you, live peaceably with all" (Romans 12:14, 18)

7

Trust Exercises

In the previous chapter I mentioned how Greg Louganis, the gold-medal diver, calmed himself before an Olympic dive by telling himself, "Even if I blow this dive, my mother will still love me." I suggested that this parallels our trust in God's grace, enabling us with God's power to live a God-centered life. But it is also true that Greg Louganis had to train rigorously. Without daily training he could not have dived so beautifully.

A pianist once said, "If I fail to practice one day, I know it. If I fail to practice two days, my friends know it. If I fail to practice three days, the whole audience knows it."

Without regular practice of putting our trust in God, our trust tends to break down, gradually replaced once again by our fears and selfishness. If fear and selfishness are our addiction, then we will need to develop habits for exercising trust. Just as a member of AA, in order to maintain sobriety, needs to turn his or her will over to God on a daily basis and attend AA meetings for mutual support, so we need various ongoing spiritual practices in order to maintain God-centeredness. These practices are usually referred to as "spiritual disciplines," but that sounds austere, as if we're punishing ourselves in order to stay in line. I think our intention is clearer if we refer to these practices as trust exercises. The point is to develop and maintain humble trust in God, shrinking our fears and self-centeredness. I will focus on five common trust exercises, though many others exist: prayer, fasting, charity, study, and community worship.

Prayer

Of all trust exercises, prayer is the most essential and seemingly the most useless, the easiest and the hardest, the most obvious and the most illogical. It is the most straightforward way in which we turn ourselves over to God, and yet, of all the trust exercises, it is the least practical in terms of immediate visible results. It is our most personal communication, and yet it is sometimes like talking to a brick wall. It is sacred time and yet is often regarded as a waste of time. Prayer embraces the paradoxical command, "Don't just do something—stand there." Or, in the words of Martin Luther, "I have so much to do that if I didn't spend at least three hours in prayer I would never get it all done."[1]

I am no Martin Luther. (Even Martin Luther was no Martin Luther— he got way behind on his daily prayers.) I practice prayer at a mostly basic level, and the many times I have tried to expand my prayer life have often not lasted very long. We each bring our own personality type to prayer, with the result that we each find different kinds of prayer meaningful. One size does not fit all. That being said, let me share some of the basics that I have learned. I will divide prayer into four types: praise, confession, petition, and silence.

Praise. At the heart of prayer is gratitude. There would be no reason to pray if we were not already grateful for what God has given us. If we see God as a force that we need to manipulate or coerce to do something for us, then we are not beginning with gratitude and we are not praying—we are practicing magic. Prayer does not begin with "I want," but with "Thank you."

At the beginning of each work day, as I sit at my desk, I look out the window at the sunshine or clouds or rain or snow and I say, "Thank you, God, for this day." Each moment of my life is a gift. There is no reason why I must exist. There is no reason why anything must exist. It is all pure gift. Saying "thank you" at the beginning of each day is a small reminder to myself of this simple, profound fact. It helps to place me in an attitude of awe rather than an attitude of taking life for granted, in an attitude of gratitude rather than an attitude of indifference. Why trust God if we are not first grateful to God? So prayer begins with and facilitates this sense of gratitude.

Before I eat breakfast, lunch, or supper, I say, "Thank you, God, for this food." Other than air, I suppose food and water are our most essential physical requirements for survival. Sustenance is also, usually, a very pleasurable

---

1. Quoted in Dawn, *Morning by Morning*, 242.

experience, a simple wonder on our taste buds and in our stomachs. Saying "thank you" is an acknowledgment of this gift that I, as a regularly well-fed person, would otherwise take for granted. It also reminds me that God is present as I'm eating, so God becomes a guest with me as I eat. The meal becomes, in a subtle way, a spiritual experience. Since I have three meals a day, it's a simple way to remind myself frequently of God's grace.

When I have a meal with those who do not practice prayer before eating, I do not express my thanks to God out loud, I simply say it within. I do not wish to impose my practice on others, or make them uncomfortable, or show off. As Jesus said, if we pray in order for other people to see us praying, then the purpose of prayer is defeated. It is to nurture a humble, grateful spirit, not a prideful one.

In the evening, before going to bed, I sometimes consider how good my life is. I then thank God for my family, my friends, my home, and my occupation. Occasionally I remind myself to thank God for the people I don't like. Maybe by so doing I will learn to appreciate them. Even if I don't, I will at least nurture an attitude of caring toward them, realizing that God made them and loves them.

In addition to saying thank you with simple words, it is a wonderfully expansive experience to sing praise to God. As the saying goes, "He who sings prays twice." Songs use words more poetic than my own, and the melodies conjure emotions of joy and yearning, wonder and humility. If I try to praise God with my own words, it usually sounds flat and stilted to me. Music does it better, and songs provide a wide scope of thanks: for nature, relationships, human abilities, the biblical story, and for God being God. If we are too self-conscious to sing alone, then in a congregation we can sing with others—and then the songs sound even better.

Dance can also be a prayer of praise. Rather than relying on language to express our "thank you," we can use the movement of our bodies. Physical movement gets God out of our heads and into every other part of our being.

The hardest test of praise is whether we can say "thank you" to God in the times of great difficulty and pain, even in the face of death. Is our gratitude contingent on always receiving what we want? Can we trust God when all goes wrong? In the valley of the shadow, gratitude will provide the light we need.

By frequently saying "thank you" to God throughout the day, every day, we make all of our actions, even physical pleasures, God-centered instead of self-centered. We make sacred anything that is done with genuine gratitude in our hearts. An attitude of gratitude defeats the mindless self-ishness and fear that cause so much harm to humanity. Out of this gratitude naturally springs the daily cry of trust, "God, I give you my will and my life."

Confession. The fourth step in the AA program is to make "a searching and fearless moral inventory" of oneself, preferably writing it all down, and then the fifth step is to share that moral inventory with another human be-ing. We cannot become whole human beings, and we cannot maintain trust in God, if we are not being honest about ourselves. Socrates said the un-examined life is not worth living. Our self-examination is never complete or entirely accurate—we cannot get outside of ourselves for an objective look—but the more honest we can be with ourselves, the more we can turn over to God.

Fairly often I am reminded of my shortcomings. When I realize I need to address a hurtful behavior or attitude, I try to be as frank with God as possible about my character flaw, and try to figure out why I keep perpetu-ating that flaw. While I'm at it, I sometimes list off as many of my various character flaws as I can think of or see. My goal is not to wallow in guilt and shame but to see the connections and patterns and be honest with myself; I may even laugh at myself. I place each flaw in God's hands, asking for mercy, and for guidance and strength. I sometimes wait in silence to see if a new approach comes to my mind that I had not thought of before (or been too reluctant to try). Confession to God leads to a more full and honest confession with others—particularly those we have wronged.

Confession should go beyond listing our defects to also include nam-ing the emotions within us. Just as communication with others is hampered when we do not get out in the open the feelings that are interfering with our relationship, so it is when we relate to God. We may be reluctant to tell God we are angry, or doubtful, or fearful, or indifferent, or bored, or ashamed, or depressed. But as we express these feelings to God they have less power over us and they interfere less with our communion with God.

The problem with confession is that it can become either a thoughtless routine, on the one hand, or an exercise in hopeless frustration, on the other. Most of our basic character flaws will be with us throughout our lives no matter what we do or how much we pray. So the goal of confession is not for us to become morally perfect (which won't happen), but morally and spiritually aware. We are being honest for the sake of being honest. We are remembering that we are in need of healing and that we are not God. By putting it into words and expressing it to God, that awareness takes an important step forward, and we are cultivating trust in God as well as humility.

Because I easily tire of my own words, I find it helpful to read aloud prayers of confession that can be found in prayer books or the back of some hymnals. These prayers of confession help me to see what I on my own cannot see, and to put into words what I have not been able to say. They open up vistas that have been clouded by my own personality, expanding the examination of my life and the expression of my feelings.

Petition. Most people assume prayer is all about asking God for things we or others need. Though this is one of the essential elements of prayer, we need to be careful, because this is where prayer becomes the most dangerous. First of all, it's dangerous because we often ask for the wrong things, slipping back into selfishness or reacting out of fear. Second, asking for things is a kind of one-way communication that, over time and by itself, becomes unsatisfying and immature. On the other hand, there's an opposite danger: we sometimes shrink from prayers of petition because we think God can't or won't respond to prayer.

Despite these dangers, petition is the meat and potatoes of prayer (or whatever your main vegan dish is!). The prayer Jesus taught his disciples is entirely petitions; it contains no thanks and only an implied confession. The petitions are as follows: may your name be honored, may your kingdom come, may your will be done on earth, give us our daily food, forgive us our sins as we forgive the sins of others, and do not lead us into temptation but rescue us from evil. One of the striking features of this prayer is that all of these petitions revolve around God being God. God's kingdom is the focus, and all our requests must fit into the pattern of that kingdom. Necessary food, reconciliation among people and with God, and not being overwhelmed by evil and its temptations are all central concerns of God's kingdom. Our own goals and dreams are absent. It is not God who submits to us but we who submit to God.

In the Gospel of Matthew, before Jesus teaches his disciples how to pray he tells them not to pile up empty phrases as if God will pay more attention because of their many words. He then reminds them, "for your Father knows what you need before you ask him" (Matthew 6:8). This raises a crucial issue and the biggest problem a lot of people have with prayer: If God already knows what we need before we ask, why ask? If God already loves us and wants to give us the good things we need, what is the point of our petitions? If we can't influence God through our prayers, why ask for anything at all?

This is where many of us have been making a wrong assumption about prayer. We think prayer is somehow a way to influence or convince or motivate or change God. It is not. Prayer does not change God, it changes us. Even prayers of petition are not for changing God but for changing us. By praying for the things God wants we strengthen and clarify our mission. When we pray for another's well-being we are inculcating a deeper love for that person and becoming more aware of our own role in bringing help. Prayer opens up space in us and in others for God to come through. We are not persuading God to act; we are opening up room in ourselves and others for God to act.

Through prayer we are replacing self-centeredness with other-centeredness and God-centeredness. This changes us so that now we are partnering with God to energize a field of wholeness. God's grace and our trust bring together a circuit of spiritual power in the world. Jesus certainly believed that God's power is made available through trust, and without trust we are closing off avenues to God's healing. Jesus' healing ministry was based on this premise.

But when we pray for those who are ill or distressed, they may not become well. Indeed, a greater tragedy may occur. In such cases was our trust insufficient? Was God's will different from what we thought it would be? No. Such questions reveal that we have misunderstood the goal of prayer. Though we often pray that others may be rescued from this or that particular circumstance, the heart of our prayer is that they—and we—trust in God no matter what happens. The ultimate healing is to rest in God's arms and pursue God's will, not to be rescued from a particular difficulty. Consider Jesus' own prayer on the night of his arrest: he asked God three times to rescue him from death, but he ultimately prayed for God's will to be done instead of his own. Trust and renewed commitment is answered prayer.

It is not we who persuade God, it is God who persuades us. Indeed, God is constantly at work persuading all of creation, moving it all toward its proper fulfillment without coercion or imposition. Our human will and the processes of nature are given freedom to choose. When we choose to pray it is we who are changed, not God. When we are changed, then God's kingdom can come and God's will can be done.

Silence. The Gospels tell us that Jesus would sometimes leave his disciples so that he could go off by himself to pray to God for long hours. Since

Jesus warned against thinking God hears us based on how much we talk, what was Jesus doing in those long private prayers? The most likely answer is that he was praying in silence. This is prayer at its most sublime. Words are put aside so that all attention is on one thing: being with God.

There are many types of silent prayer. One common type is centering prayer. Before beginning a verbal prayer of praise, confession, or petition, one becomes present to God by clearing the mind and emotions of other distractions. A simple technique is to slowly breathe in, and then count each time you breathe out. By the time you get to ten you will likely be more relaxed and your mind will not be preoccupied by other thoughts. This technique can be enriched and extended for a long period by breathing in God's love (or gentleness, peace, courage, joy, etc.) and breathing out one's fears or selfish behaviors. When you feel at rest and without worry, you then are ready to speak with God.

Another type of silence is to listen. After each verbal confession, listen for God's response. What do you imagine God is saying to you? After each petition, listen for God's guidance. How does God want to use your hands or your mouth to bring healing to the situation just prayed for? Stay in silence until you receive clarity or sense peace.

Another type of silence is to meditate on a verse from the Bible. Think about the verse from various angles. What questions does it pose for you? What word catches your attention? What is God saying to you through it? Let your mind and spirit soak in the words.

A final type of silence is inner silence as well as outer silence. One thinks of nothing; one listens for nothing; one is simply still. All is made empty. Insights and stray feelings are gently brushed away, perhaps with a focus word such as "peace." As one French peasant described it, "I don't say anything to God. I just sit and look at him and he looks at me."[2] One maintains this inner and outer silence for, say, ten minutes a day, slowly working up to perhaps an hour each day. MRI scans of nuns who practice meditative silence for long periods of time reveal changes in how their brains operate while praying. The daily practice of silence slowly changes us in subtle ways, shaping us into bearers of God's presence.

I once heard a story about a minister who came to Carl Jung, the famous psychoanalyst, for help. He was burned out from overwork, and his relationships with his family and friends were falling apart. Jung counseled him to reduce his workload to eight hours a day and to spend his evenings

2. Quoted in Adels, *Wisdom of the Saints*, 37.

by himself in his study. The minister complied. A week later he returned and said he felt no better. Jung asked him what he did in the evenings, and the minister told him he read books and listened to music. Jung said, "I didn't tell you to spend the evening with Mozart and Goethe, but with your-self." Aghast, the minister said, "I can't think of a worse person to spend time with." Jung replied, "Yet this is the person you inflict on others sixteen hours a day."

Prayer is spending time with ourselves and then bringing ourselves to God. It can be as easy as breathing, or it can be the most challenging activity we have ever undertaken. For beginners it seems hard because it is a sacrifice of our precious time—time that could be used watching TV or playing a game or fixing the sink or getting that report done. Prayer represents God asking us for a portion of our time devoted to being just with God, strengthening our trust. We resist. "It's my time and my life!" Is it? That's precisely why we pray—to remind us that it is not our time and it is not our life; it is all God's.

Fasting

Fasting is the forgotten trust exercise—at least in most of American cul-ture. Skipping meals for God makes no earthly sense to us. Besides, it is distinctly uncomfortable, and anything uncomfortable doesn't have a ghost of a chance of ever catching on. Indeed, the fact that it involves voluntarily and purposely doing something uncomfortable to oneself puts fasting in the same category as self-flagellation—surely the result of an unstable mind (or so the popular thinking goes).

And yet fasting is a widespread trust exercise, practiced through the ages by many religions, second only to prayer as a way to connect with God. The ancient Israelites fasted as part of their religion; Jesus fasted for an extended period before he began his ministry; and the religion of Is-lam instructs its followers to fast from all food and drink, from sunup to sundown, for an entire lunar month each year. There must be something significant behind this ancient practice that has made it so central to so many religions and religious leaders.

Fasting is a physical way of mirroring the spiritual act of letting go of selfishness. Food is delicious, so we all want to eat. When we eat we are normally focused on our own enjoyment. We savor the aroma of the cof-fee, the sweetness of the cinnamon roll, the flavors in the omelet. There is nothing wrong with this, particularly if we are eating with grateful hearts. But fasting is the decision to forgo this pleasure for a short time—not long enough to do us any physical harm, but long enough for us to feel the pangs of hunger. It is an act of selflessness, a way of practicing not being focused on oneself. If the time we would normally be eating is replaced with a time of prayer, then fasting becomes a physical way of giving up our self-centeredness and practicing God-centeredness. This is what makes fasting so powerful. It is an intensification of prayer through physically acting out what is happening in prayer. We are not focused on ourselves but on God. We are willing to give up what we want for the sake of what God wants.

I am not suggesting that it is God's will that we skip some meals and suffer hunger. Rather, we are choosing to fast as a symbolic gesture to ourselves and to God that we are willing to give up our desires for God's desires. We do not know what God may call on us to give up tomorrow for the sake of doing God's will and living out God's kingdom, but through fasting we are practicing our willingness to do so, and by combining fasting with prayer we are putting some thickness behind our words, "I give you my will and my life."

Fasting is not God's weight-loss program for believers; we are not doing it to give ourselves a better figure. Dieting is certainly legitimate if we need to lose weight, but fasting should not be confused with dieting. The focus is on strengthening our trust in God, not reducing our weight.

Through fasting we learn important lessons. The first is that we have some control over the desires of the body. We don't have to stuff ourselves every time the thought of food goes through our mind. We can decide what is good and healthy for us. We learn that we can put off a small pleasure now for a greater joy later. This is crucial to the development of our maturity.

Fasting teaches us to appreciate the gift of food even more. There is nothing like the absence of food to heighten our appreciation for food. At least in our society, we take food for granted. It's everywhere: supermarkets overwhelm us with an avalanche of variety, and restaurants of every cuisine and price range make it possible for us to gorge ourselves without the tedium of preparation and cleanup. Food is so easy and available that it has lost its essential quality of being essential. Fasting helps to restore food's preciousness.

Through fasting we also learn to identify with those who are hungry. Some twenty million people die every year at least partly as a result of starvation and malnutrition. We do not think about this very often, or we would do more about trying to prevent it. Certainly if hundreds of passenger jets crashed each day we would demand change—so why do we usually accept the fact that food is not getting to those who need it? By skipping a meal or two each week we can remind ourselves of all those in the world who have much less food to eat than we have. This makes us more dedicated to Jesus' prayer for the world, "Give us this day our daily bread." Perhaps it will have an effect on our lifestyle and political choices.

Fasting has been used especially for the sake of receiving spiritual guidance when a crucial decision needs to be made. According to the Gospels, Jesus went into the wilderness and fasted for forty days ("forty days" simply means "a long time") as a way of receiving clarity before beginning his ministry. This kind of long-term fasting (one still drinks liquids) clears the mind of all other distractions so that one's focus is only on God. Going days without food sometimes induces altered states of consciousness—visions—which one may find helpful for guidance or assurance. But one does not need to fast several days in order for fasting to help provide clarity for an upcoming decision. Any length may be helpful—from one meal to three meals—and one continues this practice weekly until God's guidance seems clear. Fasting is simply a way of intensifying prayer, making it more serious through physical self-sacrifice.

So far I have treated fasting as the forgoing of food, but fasting can also be understood in a broader way: the giving up or cutting back on anything we take for granted. Because American society consumes too much meat, too much electricity, too much oil, and too many products for the sustainability of this planet, fasting from our overconsumption has become important for our moral well-being and urgent for humanity's physical well-being. We don't really want the rest of the world to have an American standard of living, because if everyone lived as most Americans do the world would quickly become a desert. So the equitable solution is for all of us to live simply.

Traditionally, the season of Lent—the six and a half weeks prior to Easter—has been a time for fasting and giving up certain foods. Lent provides us with an excellent time-period for living as simply as possible, practicing a sustainable lifestyle and intensified spiritual habits. For instance, a family might decide that during Lent it will refrain from going out to restaurants, buying new clothes, purchasing toys or luxuries, eating junk food and desserts, eating meat, drinking soda, drinking alcohol, going on trips or holidays, and watching TV. In its place, the family eats home-cooked vegetarian meals, plays family games, talks together, goes for walks and rides bicycles, reads good books, and spends more time than usual in prayer. Such a commitment might strike horror in the hearts of most Americans as a picture of religion gone mad. In reality, it is simple sanity. Much of the world lives even more simply than this. It may be the case that we will need to cultivate such a life if we want to avoid environmental collapse.

But even leaving aside the needs of the environment and the world population, living as simply as possible during the season of Lent would have significant spiritual benefits. By removing the clutter we gain perspective on what is truly needed, what gives us joy, and what is meaningful. By doing without we find our priorities and increase our gratitude. By doing this for God, we put our lives more sincerely and completely into God's hands.

This forgotten exercise in trust should be forgotten no longer. Fasting puts meat into our commitment instead of into our stomachs. But, like prayer, it must not be done for the sake of showing off or with the result of feeling superior to others. This undermines its fundamental purpose of increasing our humble submission to God. Fasting is not a competition; it is the opposite of pride. It is an act of self-emptying.

Charity

It may seem odd to think of charity as a trust exercise. We aren't explicitly relating to God when we give away money; rather, we're engaged in a concrete action of giving aid to those who need it. This sounds more like an example of discipleship—doing God's will in the world by sharing our resources. Charity is indeed an act of discipleship, of concretely living out God's kingdom. But charity also becomes a trust exercise when it is a habitual practice that helps to keep us centered on God.

In early Judaism the three great trust exercises were prayer, fasting, and giving alms. Each was seen as a spiritual habit that reinforced one's devotion to and attention on God. Giving alms was a way of taking care of the poor, and providing resources for building and maintaining places of worship and the study of scripture. It was seen as a spiritual act, honoring God. When the temple existed in Jerusalem, people also brought to the temple the first fruits of their crops and flocks. By giving 10 percent of their grain and livestock to the temple each year, and burning a portion on the altar as part of a religious ritual, they were worshiping God, offering the first and best of their wealth to God. It was one of the most fundamental ways of showing allegiance to God. The food that was offered was also a practical way to feed the priests and maintain the temple.

Today churches continue this practice of having members bring "offerings" in which money is placed in a plate or basket (rather than burnt on an altar!) as part of the worship service. Giving one's offering of money isn't simply a practical transaction for maintaining the church building and programs; it is an act of worship. The money is given "to God," often with prayer and singing.

Jesus famously said, "You cannot serve God and wealth" (Matthew 6:24). Each has the character of being master of one's life; you can't serve both so you must choose between them. About a third of all of Jesus' teachings are about money, and they all have a common theme: its power to corrupt our allegiance to God. So giving away money to those in greater need is not only a way of serving God's purposes in the world, it is also a way of lessening greed's grip on us. Greed—the desire for more—is the epitome of self-centeredness. By making charity into a regular habit, purposely divesting ourselves of some of what we have, we are establishing a trust exercise that undermines self-centeredness in its most material form.

So how much should we regularly give away? Setting an amount is arbitrary and may fluctuate according to a person's circumstances and personality. It's like asking how much we should we pray or how much we should fast—no single answer will suffice. The amount should be enough that it makes a significant impact on our lifestyle, but it should not be so much that it makes it impossible for us to meet our needs. If we take Jesus' teaching "Love your neighbor as yourself" to its logical conclusion, then we should perhaps give away all the wealth we don't need for our own survival until everyone can survive. I admit: I've never done this—I'm too selfish.

In the Old Testament, 10 percent was the expectation from each Israelite family. This amount was significant but not usually impoverishing, and it met the needs of society. Ten percent may be a good guideline for us to use as a beginning point for our own discernment. For many households in which the adults are underemployed, giving away 10 percent may be too much, making it impossible to pay for food, utilities, and mortgage. For many households in which the adults are fully employed and there are no children, 10 percent may be far less than what they could give away regularly. In any case, our goal should be a world in which everyone has enough.

A funny thing happens as we become wealthier: we often find it harder to give away 10 percent of our income. The reason for this is that as we become wealthier we set higher goals for our family's well-being. We move to a higher tier of expectations in which it is thinkable to send our children to college, save money for a comfortable retirement, have a spacious home for entertaining, drive new cars that offer extra luxuries, and travel to exotic places. These are enormous expenses, and some—like retirement plans—have no natural limit; we can just keep piling in more money. As a result, middle-class Americans on average give away a smaller percentage of their income than the lower class does. The question for us then becomes: who has our higher loyalty—our desired lifestyle or God? If the rest of the world were as well off as us we could make a case for keeping our incomes for ourselves and exercising our trust in God in other ways. But this isn't the case—not by a long shot.

The fact that many Christians stress so much over the question of what percentage of their income should go to charity (and whether the percent should be calculated on income before or after taxes) shows how strong the grip of greed is, and how much we are missing the point of charity. We want as much for ourselves as we can. Society certainly doesn't help us, since it assumes the goodness of greed. Our entire economy is based on greed, encouraging us to spend outrageous amounts on ourselves, and going into debt, well beyond anything we need. Greed, as defined by our society, means excessive desire for more. But what is excessive? Our society says it's excessive only if it leads you to criminal acts or brings about your downfall in other ways. Otherwise we are encouraged to desire as much for ourselves as possible.

Charity is needed for breaking this addiction to selfish greed. If we practice giving away a sizeable portion of our wealth each week, we may have some hope of serving God rather than money.

To whom should our charity go? If we believe that the faith community represents the hope of God's wholeness in the world, then it makes sense that most of our regular charity would go to carrying out the mission of the faith community. If it is a healthy faith community, as I have described it, then our money would be going for mutual aid, educational and spiritual needs, and reaching out to help heal the world. However, God's mission in the world surely goes beyond what our faith community is doing, and so we may also give a portion of our regular charity to other organizations that are working toward wholeness.

There are three great spiritual dangers to charity. The first is, once again, pride. It is easy for us to congratulate ourselves on all that we are giving away, or to compare our giving to others and feel spiritually superior to someone who gives less. We may even seek attention for our charity (and many institutions are glad to give it to us in the form of naming rights). This undermines the purpose of charity and corrupts it. Whatever good was accomplished through that charity has now been partially (or perhaps entirely) thwarted by the re-establishment of self-centeredness.

The second great danger is that once we have given a certain percentage of our income to charity we will be under the impression that the rest of our money may now be used for whatever personal desires we have. But this is confusing charity, which as a habitual practice is a trust exercise, with discipleship. Once we've given our charity our discipleship is not over. Our entire lives, including all of our possessions and financial resources, still belong to God and are dedicated to God's mission in the world. Even after we've performed the weekly trust exercise of charity we're going to run across people in need. Will we ignore them because "I already gave at the office"? No. As people filled with God's love, we pour out God's love wherever we see it is needed. We will surely end up giving away far more than our preset percentage for weekly charity. As Martin Luther said, "If our goods are not available to the community, they are stolen goods."[3] All we have is at God's disposal. We are not more valuable than any other human being. So we hold all of our possessions lightly, opening up our hands generously as needs arise.

The third danger is that charity can become, not an exercise in grateful trust, but a joyless obligation. If it becomes in our minds a legalistic obligation—a necessary act for pleasing God and staying in God's favor—then we are back in the original human dilemma of fear and self-centeredness. Charity no longer expresses and nurtures trust and wholeness. It would be better not to give at all than to give out of a fearful or resentful obligation. That simply makes us sicker, not healthier. In such a circumstance we need to go back to the basics, experience again God's generosity and charity toward us, and then act out of inspired gratitude.

Study

Martin Buber, the famous Jewish philosopher, said that on one occasion his grandfather, when he was old and paralyzed, was asked to recount a story about his great and holy teacher, the Baal Shem Tov. Buber's grandfather

3. Quoted in Jackson, *Quotes for the Journey*, 109.

then told about how the holy man used to jump and dance as he prayed. As he told the story he was so swept up with the memory that he began to jump and dance himself in order to show how his teacher used to do it. Suddenly, Buber's grandfather realized he was healed of his paralysis.[4]

For Christians, the biblical story is their healing story. So one of the most important habits for fostering trust in God is to hear the story, study the story, and tell the story. By doing so we become the story; the story shapes our character and brings healing to our paralysis.

The Bible is not a list of divine rules to be memorized and followed, nor is it a series of moral tales from which we learn ethical principles that we then apply to various sticky situations. One of the shocking aspects of the Bible is how immoral the main characters are! Rarely are they meant to be ethical examples for us. Rather, the biblical story as a whole—including its psalms, proverbs, philosophical reflections, and prophetic pronouncements—creates a universe of faith that tends to produce in us certain virtues and strengths. We are slowly infected with generosity, patience, kindness, humility, faithfulness, and courage. Largely absent from the heart of the Bible are classical virtues such as prudence, moderation, and reputation. The biblical story is too subversive for those sober virtues. It shapes us into something more radical, beyond the ways of the world.

The biblical story can be studied in several different ways, each of which reveals treasures that enrich our trust in God. A beginner's approach is to read the Bible in a straightforward manner. Questions of what is historical are set aside. The reader thinks of it all as true, fully entering its universe and experiencing it with wonder. Many people attempt to read the Bible all the way through, from Genesis to Revelation. But such an approach is rarely successful since most people get bogged down in the ritual laws of Leviticus, or the boundary lines of the twelve tribes of Israel, or the lengthy diatribes of the prophets. Perhaps a better strategy is to start by tracing the narrative sweep of the Bible: Begin with Genesis, Exodus, and Numbers, but feel free to skip over (for now) the rituals and legal instructions. Move on to the first eleven chapters of Joshua, then read Judges and continue through to the end of 2 Kings. Then read Esther and Nehemiah. Now move from the Old Testament to the New Testament, reading the Gospels and finishing with the Acts of the Apostles. By doing this the reader will see the entire sweep of the biblical story and better grasp what it's about.

4. Bausch, *Storytelling*, 54.

After the main narrative is completed, one can turn to other parts of the Bible and read some of Psalms, some of Proverbs, the Book of Job, and some of Paul's letters. Moving back and forth between the Old Testament and New Testament, the reader slowly covers all of the books of the Bible, but without spending so much time in one type of literature that one becomes too weary to continue. There is no hurry. If one chapter is read each day, the entire Bible will be covered in about three years. If a few parts of the Bible are never read, don't worry about it. One can feel free to go back to favorite books (or puzzling books) and read them again and again.

Inevitably, many questions will arise while reading the Bible. If one is reading the Bible with a group, these questions can be discussed together and figured out as best as the group can. A "study Bible" with extensive footnotes and explanatory articles or a commentary can be used if one wants background information or a scholarly opinion. The main point, though, is not to know what the scholarly or historical answers are; the point is to ask ourselves: What does this mean for us today? How do we live out God's intention for us? Such questions are especially fruitful when discussed in a group with members of a faith community.

A more creative direction is to engage the Bible through artistic expression. One seeks to retell the Bible through drama, video, music, art, or storytelling. Creating the artistic expression, as well as watching or listening to it, is a form of delving more deeply into the Bible. Even watching secular productions based on the Bible, such as *Godspell* or *Joseph and the Amazing Technicolor Dreamcoat*, are ways of reflecting upon the power of the biblical story.

Another approach, which should not be reserved just for priests and pastors, is a scholarly study. This kind of Bible study is best offered at a college or seminary and taught by a specialist (though a well-trained pastor could offer such a class at a church). The class examines the historical sources, the process of transmission, and the factors that shaped the final text. The culture and the political and social environment are studied in order to increase understanding. The emphasis is on what a particular book or passage meant in its original context so we can more faithfully discern what it may mean in our context. This type of Bible study is valuable for helping us get out of our own worldview and see reality the way the biblical authors did.

Finally, there is the contemplative way of studying the Bible. This way focuses on small pieces—perhaps just a paragraph or a verse—and looks for spiritual meanings that may be underneath the surface meaning. This approach is often combined with prayer and silence; in fact, the verses may be turned into prayers.

There are certainly other ways of studying the Bible, but these are perhaps the most common. All of them can be repeated endlessly, covering the same biblical passages, because we all continue growing, learning, changing, and seeing new meanings. In the process we inhabit the Bible and the Bible inhabits us, and its character and faith and virtues rub off on us and get absorbed into our spiritual bloodstream.

But studying is not limited just to the Bible. To loosen our self-centeredness and strengthen our God-centeredness, it is most helpful to widen our study to all aspects of faith, including church history, theology, ethics, and spiritual life. Each of these topics could be subdivided into many more—plenty to keep us busy for a lifetime. In addition, secular studies, when brought into conversation with our faith, are extremely enlightening and helpful: philosophy, literature, sociology, psychology, political science, economics, anthropology, biology, physics, and history. Finally, we need to study and bring into conversation current events and issues. Karl Barth, the great twentieth-century theologian, said that pastors need to preach with the Bible in one hand and the newspaper in the other. Our faith has to encounter the world deeply, and that necessitates study. Without it the faith community cannot be healthy, embracing intellectual honesty and integrating diverse truths.

I recommend engaging in study at least once a week if we are to exercise our trust in God adequately. As with all the other trust exercises, study can deteriorate into haughtiness. On the other hand, some people take pride in their ignorance. The point is not to compare with others or to think study increases our value as human beings. We study for the joy of understanding and growth, and to help ourselves more humbly serve God.

Community Worship

The trust exercise that ties all the others together and keeps them energized is community worship. Without community worship we are basically on our own, and few people can sustain and nurture genuine God-centeredness on their own. Perhaps the greatest strength of the AA program is gathering alcoholics together at regular meetings for the sake of total honesty and mutual support. This, along with the habits of the twelve-step program, is what keeps addicts sober. The gathering of the faith community is an AA meeting for all who are addicted to fear and self-centeredness. Worship is at the heart of that gathering, though all of its activities—education, fellowship, meals, and ministries—are a part of the spiritual network that keep disciples focused on God and wholeness.

The gathering of the faith community helps us practice all of the trust exercises: there is always prayer and charity and study, and sometimes fasting. Doing these trust exercises together reinforces and intensifies them. As a magnifying glass pulls together and focuses light, so does the worship of the community.

The community of worship may be as small and simple as one's own family around the dinner table, or a few friends who gather regularly for prayer and study. More frequently, the Christian faith is organized into larger congregations, numbering anywhere from a dozen to many thousand, that meet weekly. The vast variety in Christian congregations is mind-boggling. They are divided into thousands of different branches of the Christian faith, each with its own distinctive interpretations and applications of the Bible. Even within the same branch, congregations may differ radically in their style of music and the structure of their worship—from electric guitars and dancing to chanting and incense.

With a different congregation available on every major (and many minor) crossroad, how is one to decide which congregation to belong to? We rarely start from scratch. Usually we have a family member or a friend who already belongs to a congregation and who invites us to visit; or we had a parent or a grandparent who used to attend a particular branch of the Christian faith, and so we seek out one of its local congregations. Or sometimes we are impressed by the ministry of a particular congregation and we decide to visit. However we decide where to begin, the important point is to find a healthy congregation. There is no point in attending a community of faith that does not nurture wholeness.

A temptation to avoid, however, is church hopping. This is the common practice of attending one congregation for a short while until one gets bored or annoyed by something, and then going on to another congregation until the same thing happens again, and then moving on to another congregation, and another, in a never-ending process. This represents a failure to commit to community, and is a sign that self-centeredness is having its way. One cannot experience the healing benefits of community if one is unwilling to grow through the inevitable stresses of being with people who are different from oneself. Being in community is somewhat like being in marriage: one does not mature in love until one makes a commitment to stick with the relationship for better or for worse, in sickness and in health. If the faith community is truly unhealthy (not just stressful), then help it become healthy; failing that, leave. But avoid walking out on your commitment to mutual love and support simply because you're not getting your way in a disagreement. A commitment to the worshiping community is, for most people, the most powerful avenue to spiritual maturity.

There are some people who, due to their personality makeup or life experiences, are not comfortable in most social settings. They may never be active participants in a worshiping community, and yet, on their own, they may indeed maintain a vibrant and transcendent trust in God. Such people are the exceptions in our society. They remind us that human diversity does not permit a single approach to our wholeness. Nonetheless, for most of us, our trust in God grows in the context of community worship.

Once, on a plane trip, I got into a conversation about religion with a young woman seated next to me. She told me how fascinated she was by religion and how she planned to pursue a PhD in religious studies. I asked her if she belonged to any religion. She said no; she just wanted to study religion. I suggested to her that if she really wanted to study religion she should actually join in. Religion can be studied from the outside, with many fruitful insights, but it cannot be understood from the outside. One does not understand dance until one dances, and one does not understand religion until one dances within it.

8

A Healing Christian Community

In the first chapter of this book I suggested twelve characteristics of a healthy religious community. These characteristics, I believe, apply to any religion. I then focused on one religion—the Christian faith—seeking to describe the essential beliefs and practices that are consistent with fostering a healthy Christian faith. Now that we have reviewed the foundational story of the Christian faith, examined the meaning of Jesus' ministry, death, and resurrection, and explored how we and our world become whole according that faith, it is time to add twelve more characteristics as a summary. Building on the foundation of the twelve characteristics of a healthy religious community, I now suggest twelve additional characteristics of a healing Christian community:

1. *Recognizes the Bible as its grounding story.*

2. *Cultivates a vibrant faith in God.*

3. *Fosters a commitment to following Jesus.*

4. *Opens itself to the presence of God through its corporate worship.*

5. *Facilitates making a public commitment to God through Jesus, and prepares people for involvement in the mission of the church.*

6. *Uses rituals that enact core elements of the biblical story so that its members become living participants in the story.*

7. *Models God's kingdom through diversity.*

8. *Avoids mixing the worship of God with the celebration of nationalism.*

9. *Practices mutual aid.*

10. *Serves society by giving help, promoting justice, and building peace.*

11. *Serves society by being an example.*

12. *Serves society by sharing God's story and inviting participation.*

Recognizes the Bible as its grounding story. When I was about ten years old my parents gave me *The Children's Bible*, an abridgment of the Bible filled with colorful pictures on every page. I devoured it, and it helped me see "the big story." The images on its pages are still the images that most readily come to my mind when I think of various stories in the Bible. When I was a teenager I bought a copy of *Reach Out*, a breezy paraphrase of the New Testament. The story of Jesus and the letters of Paul leapt off the page, firing my imagination and making me yearn to know more. Based on this popular paraphrase, my friends and I started multiple Bible studies, and we never tired of discussing the meaning and possible applications of the passages we read together.

The Bible is the touchstone that provides the congregation with its most basic identity. All other stories are valuable but secondary. So the community's preaching and teaching must center around these scriptures by retelling, studying, and interpreting them. In many Christian educational programs the Bible is learned in isolated bits and pieces, but members also need to learn how all those pieces of the story come together to create one great story. The congregation needs to understand the Bible's inner coherence—its plot, climax, and hoped-for resolution.

Because of the rise of television, computer games, and other visual and auditory entertainment, reading books is decreasing in popularity. The Bible is a very large and complicated book, so expecting members of the faith community (especially youth) to read it is becoming increasingly difficult. The church will probably need to become more creative in the ways it enables its members to encounter the sacred story. We need more than just another modern translation or paraphrase; we may need to be handing out graphic novel Bibles to our youth, or Bible video games. We need to do more creative storytelling and dramatization of the sacred story, as well as make more use of video and other artistic expressions. Nevertheless, these other media that can be used for communicating the contents of the Bible can never replace the Bible itself; we must always find ways to get people into the primary source as well.

Other educational themes are extremely valuable supplements: church history, theology, devotional studies, discussion of current issues, etc. These must link up with the identity the congregation derives from the Bible.

Some people have suggested that the time has come for new or forgotten books to be added to the canon of the Bible. I disagree. The books that comprise the Bible—the "canon"—are unique in that they have been tested by the faith community over time, under many circumstances and in many places, for their witness to and consistency with the core biblical story. Some books of the Bible may not be as useful to the faith community as others in the canon, and some spiritual documents outside the canon may be more helpful for some people than a particular book in the Bible at this time. But altering the canon now in order to add our personal favorites or remove our least favorites would only splinter the larger Christian community. Altering the canon for the sake of our current sensibilities ignores the long view of history and human need. The Bible as a whole is wiser than any one generation or geographic locality or denominational affiliation of the church.

On the other hand, if an ancient letter written by Paul were to be discovered today, and congregations and denominations around the world found it to be extraordinarily useful, then I could imagine the canon of the Bible being opened up for this addition. But this is not likely to ever happen.

Cultivates a vibrant faith in God. An African folktale tells of a man who noticed that his herd of cows was no longer giving milk. Concluding that someone was stealing the cows' milk during the night, the man hid in some bushes. That night he saw ropes coming down from the sky and wondrous maidens descending on the ropes, carrying gourds. The maidens milked the cows and then ascended the ropes. One maiden in particular was quite beautiful, so the man ran from his hiding place and held on to the sky maiden. She struggled to get free until he said, "I wish to marry you." She replied, "I will marry you under one condition: I have a basket you must never open until I tell you to." The man agreed, so they were married, and the maiden's basket was placed near the door of their home. One day, when his wife was gone, the man's curiosity overwhelmed him and he opened up the basket. When his wife returned home she was suspicious: "Did you open my basket?" The man admitted it and apologized. "What did you see in it?," she asked. "It was empty," the man replied. The woman cried, "I cannot live with you any longer." "Why not?," asked the man. "Because the basket was not empty; it was filled with what is most precious to me—sky. In time I would have helped you to be able to see, but now it is too late. How can I live with you when what is most precious to me is emptiness to you?"

A congregation that doesn't really believe in God—doesn't actually put its trust in God so it is enabled to see "sky"—is neither Christian nor sustainable over time. Some people belong to a Christian community because they enjoy the aesthetics of worship or the comforts of fellowship or the nostalgia of a particular tradition, but for them God is secondary. A congregation made up of more than a small minority of such persons will be greatly hampered in its identity and vitality. At the heart of a congregation's trust is God's presence. God is not an abstraction or a mental construct, but is relied upon as the genuine source of all being and grace.

Fosters a commitment to following Jesus. It used to be popular for some Christians to wear wristbands with the initials WWJD—What Would Jesus Do? Often criticized as simplistic, I think the question is basically on-target. For the Christian community, the face of God is seen most clearly in Jesus. Jesus provides the ultimate focus for the Bible, and his ministry is the interpretive center for the Bible. As a result, Jesus is the ethical norm for the Christian community as well as the one who embodies God's authority and hope.

The problem with the WWJD wristbands is that most Christians do not think very deeply about what Jesus would do. They have already marginalized Jesus' most radical teachings, replacing the Jesus of the Gospels with a domesticated, comfortable, patriotic Jesus. The church needs to get back to following Jesus and truly making him Lord over our politics, economics, employment, and social relationships. We do not impose this commitment or way of life on others, but we freely choose it for ourselves.

Opens itself to the presence of God through its corporate worship. I have asked many people over the years, "At what moment in your life have you felt the closest to God?" For some it was when resolution came to a painful crisis, and for others it has been an overwhelming experience of the beauty of nature; only a few have told me that their closest moment with God was in a worship service. This is neither surprising nor alarming. Corporate worship is rarely a mountain-top experience; but it does need to be a regular refocusing and replenishing of faith.

Worship is not a religious lecture followed by taking up a collection. Nor is it a venue for musical and visual entertainment. It is primarily neither a cognitive experience nor an aesthetic performance; rather, it facilitates a relationship with God's presence. Prayer is the heart of worship. Prayer may be through various modes—singing, reciting, listening, speaking, dancing or silence—as long as it effectively connects worshipers with God's wonder and grace, and God's empowerment through the Spirit. High-church Episcopalianism and low-church Pentecostalism can both bring either an experience of God or an experience of human noise-making, depending on the sincerity and openness each worshiper brings.

Corporate worship needs to be a corporate experience, not simply a bunch of individuals gathering as strangers to have their own isolated experiences. If the church is the body of Christ (as Paul says), and if Jesus is present whenever two or three gather in his name (as Matthew 18:20 says), then worship must emphasize the bringing together of our prayers and faith and fellowship. By so doing, God is uniquely present to us.

Facilitates making a public commitment of one's life to God through Jesus, and prepares people for involvement in the mission of the church. As a youth and young adult I saw many people join the church during Sunday morning worship services. It was always perfunctory and unemotional. Then, while working in another congregation, I became acquainted with a young woman whose life of abuse and shame had led to a suicide attempt. Desperate to find a turning point, she sought out our congregation and there experienced grace, safety, and healing. After attending classes on the faith and mission of the church, she decided to join. I remember the tears of joy streaming down her face the morning she made her profession of faith and committed herself to the congregation. On that day I saw for the first time the process of real transformation.

God's grace is not activated in our lives until we turn our lives over to God in trust, so a Christian community must have effective ways to help people make this commitment. Some congregations do this through an altar call at the end of every worship service; some do it through regularly offered membership classes that culminate in a public commitment to Christ and the congregation.

The drawback to the altar call is that it asks for a quick (often emotionally based) response that is frequently disconnected from full integration into the life and mission of the congregation. One gives one's life to Jesus and then later (maybe) considers commitment to the congregation. These two should be held together as much as possible. Belonging to Christ and belonging to Christ's church go hand in hand. One lives out the mission of Jesus through the mission of the church; we create wholeness together.

On the other hand, the drawback to having one's public commitment to God follow a membership class is that it tends to turn spiritual trust into an educational process. Once one has attended the right classes and learned the correct history and doctrines, one is then allowed to say in front of others, "Jesus is my Lord," and become a member of the church. This may turn faith into doctrinal assent, draining it of its dynamic nature. This approach also misses opportunities for letting people express their faith to the congregation during times of transformation.

The ideal may be a combination of both: have multiple opportunities for people to turn their lives over to God, which then lead naturally into a discipleship training and commitment process, culminating in a public commitment to Christ and the mission of the church.

Uses rituals that enact core elements of the biblical story so that the congregation becomes living participants in the story. A few years ago I visited the ruins of Philippi, a city where Paul the apostle planted a congregation. According to the Acts of the Apostles, Paul met a woman named Lydia by the city's river, taught her the good news, and baptized her. Today, next to that river stands a church. In the very center of the church are steps—from all four directions—descending into a pool for baptism. Directly above the pool is a dome that depicts Jesus' baptism. No one can enter that church or worship there without being visually reminded of this sacred ritual and the ancient story behind it; it is literally the center of the church.

Almost all religions contain sacred rituals, and the function of the rituals is to allow the participants to enter into the timelessness of the sacred story. This is true for the Christian faith as well. Two rituals in particular are of key importance to re-enacting the story. The first is baptism. This is the entrance ritual of the Christian faith. It has various symbolic meanings: washing away sin and being forgiven, as well as death to self-centeredness and resurrection to Christ-centeredness. Baptism was experienced by Jesus himself, and the early church quickly took up its practice. By being baptized one is entering the story of Jesus' baptism, as well as older stories in the Bible of crossing through water from slavery to freedom or from the wilderness to the Promised Land. By undergoing baptism one is physically enacting what one is spiritually committing, deeply rooting that commitment.

The second ritual is the Lord's Supper (also called Communion or the Eucharist). It is based on the Gospel accounts (and Paul's account) of Jesus' last meal with his disciples before his arrest and crucifixion. The bread at the meal symbolizes his broken body, and the wine is his poured out blood. By eating the bread and drinking the wine, one is joining the original disciples at that table and is being bound to Jesus in that sacred covenant. Jesus' life and self-sacrifice are being taken into oneself; Christ-centeredness is being enacted. The meal also reminds us of all the other meals Jesus shared in which the kingdom of God was enacted by breaking bread with even the outcasts of society. Whereas baptism marks the entrance into the Christian community and its mission, the Lord's Supper is the regular replenishing of one's commitment to belong to Jesus.

In many Christian traditions the bread and wine are not merely symbols of Jesus' body and blood, but actually become Jesus' body and blood. This makes the ritual all the more necessary for believers since it becomes a direct conduit for God's saving power. Similarly, some Christian traditions believe that baptism is more than a symbol; it is the actual and only way in which our sin can be removed and we can be saved. These understandings perhaps run the risk of replacing trust with ritual, and relationship with ceremony. Is one able to genuinely trust God and become Christ-centered without undergoing baptism? I think so. Can God forgive us without our undergoing a certain ritual? The thrust of the New Testament says yes. Baptism and the Lord's Supper are public markers that aid our faith and strengthen community, but they are not God's requirements for wholeness or fellowship with God.

Some Christian communities, following the instructions of Jesus found in the thirteenth chapter of the Gospel of John, practice a ritual of foot washing. At the Last Supper Jesus washed his disciples' feet, giving them an example of being a servant. He then told them to follow this example. Christian communities that practice foot washing are physically enacting and being reminded of their commitment to humble service to one another, which is at the heart of the Christian mission.

Some Christian groups, such as the Quakers, do not believe in the use of any rituals, including baptism and Communion. Since rituals easily degenerate into magical thinking, and since true faith is a spiritual reality, they believe it is better not to use sacred rituals at all. In unprogrammed Quaker meetings worship consists of silence. In silence we are present with God and God's inner light guides us. As true as this is, I think something crucial is lost over time when the church does not practice rituals for embodying the key moments of the sacred story. Quakers have thrived for a few hundred years, but I think the universal church and our Christian identity would suffer over time if this were the dominant practice of all churches.

Models God's kingdom through diversity. For several years, on a particular Sunday each year, scores of churches throughout Indianapolis, Indiana closed their doors and instead met together downtown in Market Square Arena for worship. The service blended together the rich and the poor, Baptists and Methodists, Presbyterians and Disciples, Anglos and Hispanics and African Americans. The service blended together various worship styles and songs and rituals. It was an exciting taste of God's coming kingdom on earth.

Table fellowship with tax collectors and other social outcasts was one of Jesus' most powerful methods of enacting the presence of God's kingdom. God's grace and wholeness were extended to all. The early church understood this, and in its fellowship it gathered together men and women, slaves and masters, rich and poor. Soon the early church was breaking down one of the toughest social barriers in the ancient world—the one between Jews and Gentiles. Removing social barriers and coming together in peace and wholeness is an essential aspect of being a Christian community. When those who are wealthy fellowship separately from the poor, they tend to misunderstand the poor and become blind to some of the causes of poverty. The same happens when Anglos, Latinos, Asians, and African Americans worship and fellowship separately from each other. Distance breeds distrust and misunderstanding. The social problems of society cannot be solved by one ethnic or economic group working them out on its own. We have to worship together, work together, and truly love one another.

Many churches purposely target one thin demographic slice of the total population, because if everyone in the congregation has the same cultural habits and assumptions there is less potential friction and more potential growth. Birds of a feather flock together. Certain demographics are particularly appealing: a congregation of middle-class couples in their thirties will likely attract more, and their incomes and children will keep the congregation afloat for many years.

But this is not God's wholeness in action; this is self-interest. Every Christian congregation, if it is faithful to Jesus' vision, has a mission to break down barriers and actively include as much diversity as possible. Our unity is in Jesus' vision for God's kingdom, not in our race or occupation or political affiliation.

Diversity is probably the hardest goal for a congregation to achieve. We live in a highly segregated society—racially, economically, culturally. Churches are voluntary organizations, so people will go where it is easiest and most comfortable. So diversity in a congregation cuts against the American grain and challenges basic human nature. This puts the message of the New Testament to a crucial test. Of course, many congregations cannot have racial diversity because their larger communities do not have racial diversity. But whatever diversity does exist in the larger community should ideally be reflected in the congregation as well.

Bringing together blue collar and white collar, Democrats and Republicans, seekers and believers, the sinners and the saints—this is a great challenge, and a great realization of the good news when it happens.

Avoids mixing the worship of God with the celebration of nationalism. Whenever war breaks out one can always count on a wave of patriotism sweeping through American religious institutions. Bible publishers put out Bibles with the American flag (or camouflage!) on the cover. Congregations begin singing the national anthem or saying the pledge of allegiance to the flag in worship. Although understandable, all of this represents a critical loss of clarity about our mission and our faith.

Many governments in our world provide their citizens with the great benefits of democracy, civil rights, and justice, and they should be celebrated for doing so. But such celebrations should not be confused with the worship of God and the basic mission of the church. Christian communities are to be embodiments of the kingdom of God, and the kingdom of God is of a very different character than the nations of this world. National governments serve their own national interest, and they do so through the use of enforced laws and, if need be, war. In contrast, the kingdom of God knows no national boundaries and concerns itself equally with all people, pursuing its mission without the use of harm. No nation reflects the kingdom of God, so no nation should be celebrated as part of the congregation's worship of God. Governments are to be respected. Certainly one may take pride in one's nation and its good accomplishments, but this should never be wedded to the worship of God.

Patriotism and religion are a powerful mix. Each appeals to deep emotions and loyalties. No wonder many churches have actively brought the two passions together to feed off of each other and generate exponential energy in the congregation. But such a course is disastrous to our faith. It turns the Christian faith into a civil religion that promotes the nation's self-interest. The kingdom of God is too big for that, and the church must be free to critique the nation from the perspective of God's justice—a justice that calls for all governments to stand up for those with the least power.

The church is a foreign embassy for the kingdom of God. Each congregation is situated within a particular nation, but the soil upon which that congregation meets is, spiritually speaking, not the soil of the host nation, but the soil of God's kingdom. The Mexican national anthem is not sung in the American embassy, and the American flag is not displayed in the Mexican embassy. An embassy keeps its identity and primary loyalty clear, and so must the church.

Practices mutual aid. In one of my congregations most of the members met together once or twice a month in small groups for a meal, fellowship, and personal sharing. If anyone within the group was hospitalized, the others often arranged for meals to be brought to the family during the recovery time. If anyone within the group was moving, the others helped pack and load the truck. If anyone was in financial need, the group pooled its resources, or referred the need to the elders of the church who administered a fund to meet all emergency needs within the congregation.

The Acts of the Apostles describes the early believers pooling their resources so that all the physical needs in their fellowship could be met. This too is an essential element of Christian community, because it's another basic way in which the congregation enacts God's healing kingdom. If we love one another, we extend ourselves (and our resources) to meet the needs of one another. A congregation should have a way in which the members pool together resources to meet each other's financial emergencies and other practical needs. Childcare, moving assistance, and meals for the temporarily disabled are just some of the practical ways that a congregation can put love in action and help bring wholeness to the group. No one should be in desperate need while others in the congregation have more than enough; this represents a failure to be a community of love and mutual support.

As a community that builds friendships together, the members are in the best position to understand the nature of each other's practical needs and the most realistic ways to help meet those needs. Mutual assistance within a community is usually more effective than assistance to those outside the community, which is one reason for trying to bring in as many people as possible. By knowing each other and relating to each other on a regular basis, the community can discern how best to help each other and reduce the risk of abuse by those receiving help. By helping one another in essential and practical ways, and being responsible for each other, we build up a community of mutual encouragement in which all are valued as equals. Mutual aid within community is the best way to provide sustained and comprehensive wellness.

Serves society by being giving help, promoting justice, and building peace. Brian Stewart, an award-winning Canadian journalist, changed his mind about the relevance of the Christian faith after experiencing first-hand the church in action: "I've never reached a war zone, or famine group or crisis anywhere where some church organization was not there long before me . . . sturdy, remarkable souls usually too kind to ask 'what took you so long?'"[1]

A healing church offers concrete assistance to those in society who are in need. Frequently this includes emergency financial aid, shelter, clothing, and food for those who cannot be adequately helped by whatever systems society has set up. The church provides a safety net, with personal care and attention, to supplement society's safety net. Congregations create needed ministries for the larger community such as job-training, housing, day care centers, fair-trade stores, home repair, etc. In addition to running their own programs, congregations send passionate volunteers out into their communities to help in schools, hospitals, and food pantries. A healthy and healing Christian community is a practical asset to the quality of life in their larger communities.

But congregations do more than simply provide aid and resources; they also promote justice and equal treatment for all members of society. A major theme in the biblical story is God's insistence that nations must protect the vulnerable and provide justice for the weak. This became a central principle for the creation of Israel. The church takes this principle to every nation, advocating for basic human rights and for all governments to live up to their own highest ideals of justice.

In a world where the barbarity of war is nearly constant, the church brings another biblical principle: care about your enemy's legitimate needs and put a priority on resolving conflict. Christian communities call on their governments and societies to interrupt the escalation of violence with

---

1. Stewart, "Christians Are on the Front Lines of Compassion."

surprising, positive action. Put as much energy and resources into building peace as preparing for war. The healing Christian community sends out its members to be a nonviolent presence in places of tension, shining a light on hidden atrocities and serving as trusted negotiators.

Serves society by being an example. One of the primary reasons why ethical change is so hard in the world is because the world believes change is not really possible. We are stuck in dysfunction and violence because of inertia and a lack of imagination and hope. Christian congregations meet this challenge by providing an example to the larger community of how community can be done in a healthier way.

The larger community, impressed by what it sees congregations doing, may decide to copy those aspects of the Christian community it finds most appealing and useful. For instance, governments, public institutions, and private companies may decide to implement servant leadership or methods of caring conflict resolution. Even if these other communities do not adopt trust in God's grace as the motivating starting point, they can still be inspired by and imitate some of the church's best practices. It was churches that started the first hospitals; now all of society has adopted this caring practice. It was churches that first provided public education—an idea embraced by many governments that has greatly enhanced equality in society.

Serves society by sharing God's story and inviting participation. To maximize its healing mission in the world, the church should not be content with merely retaining its own children, but should invite the larger community to join the healing Christian community. The church reaches out by sharing its sacred story. With respect for the faiths of others in the larger community, the church tells its story in natural, humble ways. In some countries this is not possible without provoking violence and persecution, but in places that enjoy freedom of religious expression the church should not hesitate to share its story. But if the church is not embodying the healing story and experiencing wholeness, its testimony is hypocritical and undermining the good news. I hope such unhealthy Christian communities remain silent.

No congregation fulfills all twelve of these characteristics all of the time. These are signposts for the journey. But to be a healing Christian community I think we need to be moving in these directions. Genuine Christian communities are in the process of working out the most faithful ways of pursuing God's mission. No one congregation can do everything and meet every need. This is one reason why congregations should band together—so they may become more effective communities of faith and healing, resourcing one another. Why should mutual aid be practiced only within a congregation—why not among congregations? The more we work together, the greater the wholeness we can offer the world.

The Christian faith thrives on the hope that through God's grace there is a way to bring healing to the addictions afflicting the human race. That way involves our humility and trust, our gratitude and discipleship, lived out together.

9

Other Religions and Our Ultimate Destiny

Are the scriptures and sacred stories of other religions as true and useful as those that belong to Christians? Are the faith communities of other religions also capable of bringing health and wholeness to the world? Is Jesus the only way to know God? Is faithfulness to Jesus the only way to be freed from the power of fear and self-centeredness? Is reconciliation with God available only for Christians?

A final test of the healthiness and healing qualities of the Christian faith is how it understands and relates to other religious faiths. Our society is growing increasingly pluralistic, and our ultimate well-being will depend on how all of us live together and view one another.

Imagine that before us stands a mountain. The top is shrouded in the mystery of God and the solution to humanity's woes. At the base of the mountain we see several different paths that appear to ascend the mountain. Each path represents a different religious faith. Which one should we take? Does it matter? Here are five different Christian views:

Only one path—the Christian path—will successfully take us to the top of the mountain. All the other paths are faulty paths. They may ascend for a while but eventually travelers will either come to insurmountable road blocks or the paths will meander away from the summit.

The Christian path is the most direct route to the top of the mountain. The other paths are not as good as the Christian path. Some paths get to the top of the mountain by a more circuitous or difficult route, while other paths perhaps never arrive at the top at all.

All of the paths are equally useful for arriving at the top of the mountain. All of the major world religions have proven themselves to be capable of arriving at the top of the mountain. One should choose the path that is the most appealing to one's personality or background.

Each path goes up a different peak in the same mountain range. A closer look reveals that there is not just one mountain but a mountain range with many peaks. Each religion is a path up to a different peak. For the Christian faith, the peak is God-centeredness and trust leading to wholeness. For Buddhism the peak is freedom from suffering and achieving a state of nirvana. For Taoism the peak is harmony with nature. For Confucianism the peak is good social order. Different religions are after different—though related—goals, so their paths should be judged by how well they achieve their own desired peak.

None of the paths—including the Christian religion—successfully reach the top of the mountain. All religions are faulty human constructs, and none of them reach God. God and wholeness come to us when we surrender and meet God in the valley.

Except for the first view, these are not necessarily exclusive views. We can combine different views together. For instance, it is possible to believe the Christian faith is the most direct route to wholeness (second view), and also affirm that each religion has somewhat different goals (fourth view), while at the same time recognize that all of our religious efforts are flawed so we need to humbly rely on grace (fifth view).

The position that is the most problematic is the first one: only the Christian faith can bring us to God and ultimate well-being. This view creates an obstacle between Christians and members of other religions no matter how loving Christians try to be. Members of other religions are viewed as ultimately lost: what they value the most deeply is finally and fatally wrong. But many Christians feel they have no choice but to embrace this view. They believe that central to the Christian faith is the insistence that only Christians can be rescued from sin and death. They base this position on several different verses in the New Testament. Following are three typical examples:

> . . . we know that a person is justified not by the works of the law but through faith in Jesus Christ. And we have come to believe in Christ Jesus, so that we might be justified by faith in Christ, and not by doing the works of the law, because no one will be justified by the works of the law. (Galatians 2:16)

> This Jesus is "the stone that was rejected by you, the builders; it has become the cornerstone." There is salvation in no one else,

for there is no other name under heaven given among mortals by which we must be saved. (Acts 4:11–12)

Jesus said to him, "I am the way, and the truth, and the life. No one comes to the Father except through me." (John 14:6)

The traditional way to interpret these verses is to say that unless you become a Christian, publicly claiming Jesus as the Lord of your life, you cannot be saved from destruction and separation from God. But these verses don't actually say that. In order to see these verses in a different light, we should consider other passages in the New Testament that give us a wider perspective.

Paul, the great advocate of the principle that we are made right with God through faith in Jesus, says in his letter to the Christians in Rome that God "will repay according to each one's deeds: to those who by patiently doing good seek for glory and honor and immortality, he will give eternal life" (Romans 2:6–7). That sounds as if Paul is saying that our goodness is the ultimate factor in determining our eternal fellowship with God. That's not the usual way Paul is interpreted! But just a few verses later he makes a similar point when he says, "When Gentiles, who do not possess the [God-given Jewish] law, do instinctively what the law requires, these . . . are a law to themselves. They show that what the law requires is written on their hearts, to which their own conscience bears witness; and their conflicting thoughts will accuse or perhaps excuse them on the day when . . . God, through Jesus Christ, will judge the secret thoughts of all" (2:14–16). Paul is not denying the central importance of Jesus Christ in humanity's salvation, nor is he saying that we can achieve a right relationship with God purely through our own efforts. But he does seem to be saying that one can be in a right relationship with God without specifically being a Christian.

Peter, who says that there is "no other name by which we must be saved," also says, "I truly understand that God shows no partiality, but in every nation anyone who fears him and does what is right is acceptable to him" (Acts 10:34). Peter, like Paul, is affirming that all kinds of people everywhere are capable of reverencing God and doing what is right; this is not a Christian monopoly, nor does one specifically need to be a Christian in order to be acceptable to God.

Jesus directly addresses this issue. One time he was asked, "What must I do to inherit eternal life?" According to Luke, Jesus says nothing about becoming a Christian or having faith in him. Rather, he affirms the two greatest commands in the Bible: love God with all your being and love your neighbor as yourself. "Do this," Jesus concludes, "and you will live" (Luke 10:28). Our wholeness and ongoing fellowship with God is based on turning ourselves over to God's love and living out that love. It is not based on entering a particular religion or affirming certain doctrines. To make that point clear, Jesus then immediately tells a parable about a Samaritan—a heretic who belongs to a hated religion—who demonstrates genuine love. It is the Samaritan who is shown to be living out God's love, not the leaders of the "correct faith" who failed to act with love.

Our wholeness and fellowship with God boils down to love. As another voice in the New Testament says, "Beloved, let us love one another, because love is from God; everyone who loves is born of God and knows God" (1 John 4:7). *Everyone* who loves belongs to God because God is love. All love originates with God, and love permeates all existence. Without love there is no being at all. The Gospel of John begins by saying that "In the beginning was the Word" and that all things came into being through the Word. What is the Word? It is God's self-expression that lies at the heart of God. And what is at the heart of God? Self-giving love.

The cross of Jesus Christ is the ultimate revelation of this principle. The cross is God's love revealed in its most stark, even terrifying form: God is willing to sacrifice God's own self, God's Word embodied in a human being, in order to break through our self-centered destructiveness. The cross reveals the fundamental principle that underlies all reality and is woven into every particle of existence: self-emptying, self-giving love.

Any time a person loves, he or she is tapping into that basic cosmic principle, and tapping into the cross, which reveals and epitomizes it. In other words, anyone who loves is tapping into Christ and belongs to Christ.

This is the point Jesus makes in his famous parable of the sheep and the goats. At the final judgment of humanity we will be divided into the rescued and the lost. The rescued are those who loved Jesus when he was sick and thirsty and naked and imprisoned. The rescued ask, "When did we do that?" Jesus' answer is that whenever they did it to the least person, "you did it to me" (Matthew 25:40). Our ultimate rescue is based on whether we love others, and by loving others we are, unwittingly, loving Jesus. Thus, there is little if any ultimate difference between "faith in Jesus" and loving others.

A final note about being saved through "faith in Jesus." In the Greek language in which Paul wrote, he literally says, "faith of Jesus." We are saved not by *our faith in Jesus*, but by *Jesus' faith in God*. It is Jesus' humble trust, enacting God's complete love, that ultimately rescues humanity from its self-destruction. Any time we turn from self-centeredness to God-centered love, we are connecting with Jesus' faith in God.

C. S. Lewis, the famous Oxford professor and Christian writer, summed up his understanding of what the New Testament says on this subject this way: "We do know that no [one] can be saved except through Christ; we do not know that only those who know Him can be saved through Him."[1] In other words, the claim of the New Testament is that God is offering forgiveness and healing to the world through the self-giving love and sacrifice of Jesus Christ. But that does not mean that every person who has been joined with God through Christ's self-giving is aware of Jesus Christ.

God is saving the world through Christ whether the world knows it or not. All those who live by love, whether atheist or Muslim, agnostic or Christian, are being saved by grace through faith. As the Letter of James insists, there is no divide between faith and doing good; they are the two sides of the same coin. Those who are living lives of genuine care for others are also living lives of genuine faith because they are implicitly trusting in something greater than themselves that cannot be proven.

This leads to an important question: do we need religion (any religion) to participate in wholeness and experience salvation? For some individuals who have been gifted with sharing genuine love, no. And yet the Christian faith (as well as most other religions) offers something that is essential for most people and for humanity as a whole: a faith community empowered by transcendent love that supports us and makes salvation into a social reality.

If my children were to tell me they no longer believe in God, I would be heart-broken—not because I would fear they are outside of God's eternal embrace, but because they would be hindering their access to experiencing God's healing love through trust and the community of faith.

We do not need to decide who is a part of God's salvation and who is not. Indeed, we are explicitly told by Jesus not to make that judgment: "Do not judge, and you will not be judged; do not condemn, and you will not be condemned" (Luke 6:37). Jesus tells us in parable after parable that God's judgments cannot be anticipated or manipulated. "[M]any who are first will be last, and the last will be first" (Matthew 19:30). We are not to concern ourselves with deciding the destiny of others but to focus on our own discipleship. If Jesus is "the way, and the truth, and the life" (John 14:6), that

---

1. Lewis, *Mere Christianity*, 55.

means he makes that decision—not us or our religions. Indeed, presuming to know who is truly saved and who is not saved inevitably leads to spiritual pride, the opposite of humble trust in God.

But if a person does not need to become a Christian to be rescued by God, then why share the Christian faith at all? Isn't the entire mission of the church undermined? Of course not. Those who have experienced the healing love of God through the story and community of Jesus naturally share that story and community with others. If we indeed experience good news then we will want to share it with anyone who is needing and wanting good news. We share the Jesus story because we experience it as the clearest expression of God's healing love. If others don't experience it that way, let them be. If we have taken medicine that works wonderfully for us, we tell others about that medicine. But if others don't want to hear about that medicine, we respect their wishes.

In humility we are open to understanding whatever healing others have experienced in other ways. We may even find our own Christian faith clarified and deepened by truths learned through other religions. If the Christian faith is true then it will naturally do well in the marketplace of faith and ideas. We can learn from others while also sharing what we've discovered to be true and good for us. As many have said, Christian evangelism is simply one hobo telling another hobo where he or she can find a soup kitchen.

For those who have no healing community, I readily invite them into mine. For those who have never heard the story of Jesus and want to hear it, I readily tell the greatest story I know. For those who have no sense of God's grace, I readily share the God who loves us all. But I have no need to argue or try to convince. Healing truth emerges on its own.

Once there was a man who had a magic ring. Whoever wore the ring would experience a life of wholeness. When the man lay on his deathbed his three children gathered at his side, and each asked for the magic ring. What could the man do? So he ordered that two identical copies of his magic ring be made. Then he took all three rings in his hands and shook the rings around until he no longer knew which one was the magic ring. Then he handed out the three rings to his children. "I do not know which of you has the magic ring," he said. "It will perhaps become evident as you live the rest of your lives."

And now a word about hell.

Salvation refers to being rescued from whatever imperils individuals, the human community, and all of creation. In this life salvation means a world of reconciliation, joy, health, and love. In an ultimate sense salvation means rescue from the oblivion of death, being in the fellowship of God, and participating in a new creation. But does salvation, in its ultimate sense, also mean being rescued from hell? The Christian faith has traditionally taught that those who are not part of God's eternal fellowship go to hell, a condition of eternal punishment and separation from God. Is there such a thing as hell?

The concept of hell is not found in the Old Testament. The general belief of the authors of the Old Testament is that after death everyone goes to Sheol, a place under the earth without memory or praise of God. Sheol does not represent nonexistence, but existence at its lowest level. It isn't punishment or pain, but more like dreamless sleep or suspended animation. Most of the Old Testament writers assume that Sheol has no end and there is no return from Sheol; but a few statements in the last writings in the Old Testament suggest that at least some will be raised from Sheol and given transformed lives with full existence once again.

The New Testament was written a couple of hundred years later than anything in the Old Testament, and by that time the belief had developed among most Jews that there would be a resurrection of the just at the end of history, and punishment for the wicked. This is the belief that generally underlies the New Testament. For instance, Jesus teaches that some will go into "life" and some will go to "destruction." He refers to this place of destruction as "Gehenna," which was Jerusalem's city dump. He warns that those who do not enter the kingdom of God may, because of their sins, be thrown into Gehenna, "where their worm does not die and the fire is never quenched" (Mark 9:48). This may all be figurative language based on Jerusalem's city dump, where fires always smoldered and maggots proliferated, but it still reflects an actual expectation of some kind of destruction or punishment after death.

In the Gospel of Matthew the punishment following death is more explicitly an eternal punishment. Those who do not offer help to those in need are cursed: "Depart from me into the eternal fire prepared for the devil and his angels" (Matthew 25:41). This idea of eternal punishment is found as well in the Second Letter to the Thessalonians (perhaps written by Paul, though this is disputed by scholars), in which the Lord Jesus returns to inflict "vengeance on those who do not know God and on those who do not obey the gospel of our Lord Jesus." The author says, "These will suffer the punishment of eternal destruction, separated from the presence of the Lord and from the glory of his might" (2 Thessalonians 1:8–9).

Most of the rest of the New Testament is vague about what happens after death to those who have rejected God's will. Paul sometimes refers to "those who are perishing" without elaborating on what that means. The Gospel of John similarly refers to "perishing," but without description. Taken together, the New Testament actually says very little about what we commonly call "hell." It is assumed, but not elaborated upon.

The Book of Revelation, as it describes its vision of God's final judgment, makes an intriguing statement about Hades, another name for a place of torment after death. After all of the dead are brought up out of Hades and judged, those whose names are not found in the book of life are thrown into "the lake of fire." Then "Death and Hades" are "thrown into the lake of fire" (Revelation 20:14). What does this mean? What is the lake of fire? Is hell thrown into hell? The author immediately tells us, "This is the second death; the lake of fire." The author is apparently suggesting that Hades, the place of torment for the dead, is only temporary. At the end of history, death and the place of the dead are themselves destroyed. The lake of fire is an ultimate destruction. Perhaps nonexistence is what is meant, since from now on there will be no such thing as death or Hades, only a new heaven and a new earth.

We have to be careful not to take too literally these various images of hell/Gehenna/Hades in the New Testament and recognize that they are all highly metaphorical and unsystematic. There is no one coherent and consistent picture of life after death in the New Testament (whether for the rescued or the unrescued). So what can we say about hell that is consistent with the overall message of the New Testament? Is there such a thing as hell? Or is this an idea that we should now discard?

If we mean, is there a God-imposed eternal punishment of pain for those who fail to do God's will, then I think the answer must be no. Such a hell would be impossible to square with the Bible's insistence on God's gracious, merciful, patient, and just character. But let me suggest three possible ways of thinking of hell that I think are consistent with the New Testament and life's experience:

Hell is on earth. To say there is no hell is to fail to see the true state of the world in many places and situations. Just as the kingdom of God is breaking into this world now, so is hell. Just as people are able to enter

God's kingdom while living here on earth, so people enter hell while here on earth. Hell is quite real. It is our self-destruction and our destruction of others. It is sucking the hope out of the world by perpetuating systems of poverty, violence, and oppression. Gehenna is here. We enter the trash heap of the world on a broad and easy road. But it is possible to trust God and take the narrow way that leads out of the city dump.

Hell is choosing self-absorption and isolation over the community of God's love. God does not force us to trust in God's grace. God cannot compel humility and gratitude on us. Replacing self-centeredness with self-giving needs to be our response, not one imposed on us, or we are merely robots, not people of love. After death, if we continue to have the capacity to love then it must continue to be a free response. Hell, then, is the freedom not to respond to God's love with love. If trust must be our own response then self-worship must also be our own response. Hell is not a punishment imposed but a banishment chosen. Hell is our ongoing choice not to be in God's fellowship, not to respond with humility and gratitude, not to join the community of love. C. S. Lewis imagined hell as individuals moving ever farther apart and away from God, despite God's invitation to come back. Hell is God giving us our human freedom, even after this life.

Hell will wither away as God's persuasive grace ultimately prevails. God respects our freedom to respond or not respond to God's grace, but the persuasiveness of God's grace will ultimately prevail over all our self-centeredness and fears. Hell, the place of rebellion against God's love, will eventually be empty. This hope of God's universal salvation is scattered about the Old and New Testaments, from the visions of Isaiah to the mysteries seen by Paul. In one of his letters, Paul foresees the day when the Lord Jesus will come and rule over the earth until every spiritual power in rebellion to God's grace is overcome: "When all things are subjected to [Christ], then the Son himself will also be subjected to the one who put all things in subjection under him, so that God may be all in all" (1 Corinthians 15:28). Human rebellion will eventually give way to God's grace so that God is everything to everyone.

And now a word about heaven.

It is common for Christians to talk about "going to heaven" after they die. But this may give the wrong impression of what the Bible actually anticipates. Rather than imagining ourselves "going to heaven" after death, to live eternally as disembodied spirits amongst wispy clouds, it would be more biblical for us to imagine ourselves as being in a state of waiting for God's new creation. God wants to redeem and heal the universe—people, animals, and nature itself. Our proper destiny is not a ghostly existence in a spirit realm or an absorption into a ball of light and love. Our proper destiny is the universe fulfilled. God created the universe good, and God desires for it to fulfill its goodness. When God's story of humanity's growth and wholeness has come to fruition, then God will restore us within a renewed creation. Until then, after our deaths, we are in what we might call God's perfect memory. (Once we are dead and in God's memory, wouldn't we also be outside the strictures of time? If so there would be no waiting.)

I do not know how to imagine this ultimate destiny of nature and humanity brought to fulfillment. Cosmological and quantum theories offer the possibility that there are virtually infinite universes, each one with different laws of nature, playing out virtually infinite possibilities. Might God's new creation be a parallel universe? Or perhaps this universe will be renewed and brought to fulfillment through processes we cannot currently imagine. Or perhaps we need to imagine a grounding reality underneath this reality that is even more directly real. I appreciate the modesty of the First Letter of John when its author says, "what we will be has not yet been revealed" (3:2).

All imaginings of our ultimate destiny are simply that—imaginings. I am doubtful that God's ultimate reality will be anything we have been able to philosophize or find through the instruments of science. Even the biblical visionaries who give us glimpses of an ultimate hope were shaped and limited by their own worldviews. Reality is greater than even they knew. What happens after death is beyond us. But if God is the origin and sustainer of the universe, and God's love is the basis of reality, then it is a small step to trust that nothing God loves is lost from God's hands. The essence of the Christian faith is to trust in God, because our deepest spiritual intuition is that God abides and God prevails. Whatever comes after our deaths, it will reflect the character of God.

10

God

Throughout this book I have talked a lot about God, but I have said little about who or what God is. It may seem strange to leave this for the last chapter. Wouldn't it make more sense to define God and give reasons for believing in God in the first chapter? I don't think so. Which comes first: thinking about God and then experiencing a community of faith, or experiencing a community of faith and then thinking about God? It seems to me the experience of the community of faith comes first. What we believe about God largely emerges from our experiences and interactions with faith communities: sacred stories, spiritual rituals, faith exercises, communal worship, and social relationships. We may have our own individual, personal spiritual experiences, but these experiences are interpreted through lenses we inherit from one or more faith communities (including our parents and family). It makes little sense to talk about God without first acknowledging our spiritual or religious experiences that have been mediated and interpreted by our faith communities.

What I believe about God has gone through the sieve of a lot of thinking and philosophizing, but it has its origins in the Christian community of faith, beginning in weekly Sunday school songs and Bible lessons, and in the prayers my family said around the dinner table and before going to bed. If I had been brought up in a Muslim home or a Hindu home, my beliefs about God would probably be quite different. So what makes me think that my concepts of God are in any way accurate? They may not be, nor need they be. It is not my concepts of God that matter; it is my relationship with God that matters. I have long had a relationship with God mediated by a religious community that has clothed my life with meaning, maturity, and wholeness. Maybe another religion would have clothed me differently but just as well; I do not know. I can witness only to what I know, what I have experienced, what I still experience.

Philosophers who try to draw conclusions about God through rational inquiry alone, without reference to personal religious experiences and the experience of a faith community, misunderstand God and how we come to know God. Martin Buber, the great twentieth-century Jewish philosopher, described two kinds of relationships: an I-It relationship and an I-Thou relationship.[1] In the former we seek objective knowledge of someone or something based on observation and reasoning. The "It" is studied and used for our purposes. But an I-Thou relationship is subjective, interactive, and based on love, which leads to a different kind of knowledge.

Several years ago a conference speaker handed me a pumpkin seed and instructed me to learn as much about it as I could in one minute. I measured it, weighed it, smelled it, and carefully noted its form. Then the speaker told me to love the seed for one minute. I thought that was a very odd instruction, but I did what I could. I looked at the seed and I cared about it. I thought about the mystery of life and growth in that seed; I pondered the graciousness of existence. Much to my surprise, I found myself feeling emotional. I had established an entirely different relationship with the seed and knew it in a new way.

Just the same, there are two ways of knowing God: in an I-It relationship or an I-Thou relationship. We can either study God and learn about God and talk about God, or we can love God and experience a mutual relationship.

Psalm 139 describes an I-Thou relationship with God: "O LORD, you have searched me and known me. You know when I sit down and when I rise up; you discern my thoughts from far away. . . . Where can I go from your spirit? Or where can I flee from your presence? If I ascend to heaven, you are there; if I make my bed in Sheol, you are there. . . . I praise you, for I am fearfully and wonderfully made. Wonderful are your works; that I know very well" (verses 1–2, 7–8, 14).

A person who is in an I-It relationship with God will misread these verses and conclude, "Look at how much this psalm tells us about God! God is omniscient, omnipresent, and omnipotent." But the psalmist is not intending to give us information about God; the psalmist is expressing a subjective relationship with God characterized by awe, mystery, and love.

---

1. Buber, *I and Thou.*

A 2014 Gallup poll revealed that 86 percent of Americans say they believe in God.[2] That number indicates an overwhelming majority, but from the perspective of a community of faith it is a pointless number. To say "I believe God exists" is to express an I-It relationship with God. We are making God into an object about which we have an intellectual opinion. Such a relationship with God is not irrelevant, but it misses the point. As the Letter of James says, "You believe that there is one God. Good! Even the demons believe that—and shudder" (2:19, NIV). God does not want an I-It relationship with us, but an I-Thou relationship. The point of the Christian faith (and of many other faiths as well) is not to believe in God but to love, trust, and hope in God. Knowing about God is not unimportant, but I doubt we can do this without first knowing God. This knowing comes through a community of faith that nurtures I-Thou relationships with God and each other.

The authors of Genesis were religious geniuses with a profound I-Thou relationship with God. Some parts of Genesis puzzle me, and some parts don't interest me, but most of it tells stories of a God who speaks to something primordial within me—a God who knows me. When Jacob pulls up a stone for a pillow and dreams of angels on a staircase connecting heaven and earth, I am dreaming with him. When he wrestles all night with a stranger who may be himself or may be God, I too hold on for a blessing and later limp away. This gracious and mysterious God who haunts the hearts of tent dwellers, making impossible promises but calling for trust, haunts my heart as well.

When I turn to the ministry of Jesus, I meet a God so intimate I am always a child at home. I know that my dad would never give me a stone if I asked for bread, so neither will my Father. With Jesus I look at the birds of the air and the flowers of the field, and, through an intuition and trust that goes beyond rational self-interest, I feel the freedom not to worry. But I also join Jesus in the garden of Gethsemane and feel his pain and terror as he prays, "Let this cup pass from me; yet not what I want but what you want" (Matthew 26:39).

The songs of the church are almost as embedded as Scripture within me. I sing of the beauty of the earth, the glory of the skies, and the love "which from our birth over and around us lies."[3] In this God-soaked world

2. http://www.gallup.com/poll/1690/religion.aspx.

3. Folliott Sanford Pierpoint, "For the Beauty of the Earth," 1864.

I experience that "in the rustling grass I hear him pass, he speaks to me everywhere."[4]

The great hymns also acknowledge the shadows and pain. In a profound paradox, I am invited to thank God that thorns remain in this world, "so that earth's bliss may be our guide and not our chain."[5] I am assured that there is a wisdom in God allowing sorrow into our present experience: "We have enough yet not too much to long for more: a yearning for a deeper peace not known before."[6]

Much of my mother's faith resides deep within me. She prayed each night for each one of us in the family, and she talked to God as one person talks to another. Always uncomfortable in social settings and around organized religion, she still desired her children to have a religious education, experience the beauty of Psalm 23, and know without a doubt that God is always looking after us. Each night she tucked me into bed and listened to me recite the prayer, "Now I lay me down to sleep . . ." I asked the Lord to keep me whether I lived or died, to bless the world, and to help me be a good boy. Though this children's prayer has now fallen into disuse because of its reference to death, it did me no harm; indeed, I found it comforting and profound.

Though less spiritual by nature than my mother, my father had great respect for religion, attended church regularly, and enjoyed the companionship there. From him I gained an appreciation for religious institutions and a sense of God that contained more awe. Though we children took turns offering the evening supper prayer, my father always said grace on the great feast days of Thanksgiving, Christmas, and Easter. Even the way he said "Gawd" was different from my mother—with majesty and formality.

Obviously, not every picture of God that I received as a child at church or at home has persisted into my adulthood. The foolish has hopefully fallen away. As the apostle Paul said when he was describing the process of spiritual growth and knowing God, "When I was a child, I spoke like a child, I thought like a child, I reasoned like a child; when I became an adult, I put an end to childish ways" (1 Corinthians 13:11). What I once took as literal I may now see as metaphorical. What I once thought was obvious is now mystery. It is common for young adults to throw out "childish faith" but then later in life discover what has been called a "second naiveté." We come

4. Maltbie D. Babcock, "This Is My Father's World," 1901.
5. Adelaide Anne Proctor, "My God, I Thank Thee," 1858.
6. Ibid.

back to the old stories and realize they are not as foolish as we thought, and that God is most profoundly known not through abstraction, but through reappropriating the images and relationships from childhood.

For over fifty years Christian congregations have shaped my faith in God. I have lived with these communities and led some of them. We have celebrated and cried together, blessed infants and buried the dead, shared food at table and ministered to those in need. Sometimes "God is in his heaven and all is right with the world," and at other times we are tossed into a pit of confusion and despair. But we experience it together, with God.

As I now try to define who God is for me, and who I understand God to be in the context of the Christian faith, certain concepts predominate. These ideas are not set in stone; my beliefs shift and develop as I continue to integrate religious tradition (the wisdom of the faith community distilled over time from its experience and reflection) with my own personal experience, information, and reason. It is my relationship with God that is of primary importance—not my definition of God. Nonetheless, these are the beliefs that have emerged:

God is creator and sustainer. Everything comes from God and God is beyond everything—the ground of all being, the sustainer of everything, without whom everything would wink out of existence. God is the basis of all creativity, of all that is new. There is no power outside of God. God is beyond all control and manipulation. God is that than which nothing greater can be imagined.

God is gracious. All that exists is gift; it is undeserved and continuously given. God is benevolent, self-giving for the benefit of all. This love is the essence of true power. God's power persuades rather than imposes, enables freedom rather than dominates. God takes the initiative to reach out to humanity, giving us unmerited favor and help. Our obedience to God is a grateful response to God's grace, not a way to obtain grace. God confronts our destructive behavior but is more merciful than we deserve, offering us second (and many more!) chances.

God desires justice. The Hebrews' experience of slavery resulted in a repudiation of the strong taking advantage of the weak. Justice means fairness, but fairness necessitates special attention to protecting the disadvantaged and vulnerable. God calls on all societies to be just, and through acting justly humanity will experience peace and well-being.

God is the healer of all. Through the power of love God seeks to heal, reconcile, and bring fulfillment to all things—humanity as well as all of nature. Possessing all time, and being outside time, God is patient. Wholeness is not hurried.

God is subversive. We cannot contain God within our thinking and theology. God, whose ways are unknowable, is subtle and unpredictable, upsetting our plans and calculations. God cannot be manipulated or used for our purposes. God often surprises us, reversing our expectations, managing to take the opposite side—even when we think we are on God's side.

To attempt to define God any further would be to increase exponentially my foolishness. God is in no category. God is neither a thing nor a force nor a person. Neither is God abstract. As I have heard theologian John Shea say, "It is not we who are concrete and God who is abstract; it is God who is concrete and we who are abstract." We, the abstractions, have no way of accurately imagining the concrete, the truly real. And yet, to consider and talk about God we need to use ideas. So I recognize that they are no more than shadows of God, or puppets on God's hands.

These beliefs perhaps rule out three conceptions of God that are attractive for various reasons, but which are not the God of Christian faith. Individual Christians may hold these views, but I believe these are not consistent with the faith that sustains the Christian community:

God is the earth, or nature, or the universe as a whole. Nature fills us with awe; its mysteries are endless, and its existence is without question. For these reasons, God as nature will always be popular. But such a God ultimately fails to be God. Nature, at least as understood by science, is amoral and meaningless. It has no moral purpose; it is mindless interactions of matter and energy. Nature religions often have capricious gods because nature is capricious. The Israelites insisted that God is moral and purposeful, and perhaps partly for this reason they insisted that God is not nature. In addition, human beings are capable of controlling and using aspects of nature; but if God is beyond all control and manipulation then God cannot be nature. Finally, based on science's current projections, the universe itself will ultimately die. Every star will burn out, and whatever life exists in the universe will cease to be. Such a God apparently dies with it.

Christian theology has sometimes been accused of being anti-nature since God is not identified with nature. But this is not accurate. From the biblical perspective, nature comes from God, is constantly sustained by God, reveals God, is loved by God, and will be fulfilled through God. Scripture is filled with delight in nature, seeing it as a source of wonder and intimations of God's presence and grace. Some Christian theologians have suggested God is *in* everything rather than *being* everything—panentheism rather than pantheism.

God is the human unconscious. According to Jungian psychology, the unconscious is where wisdom, healing, and every spiritual resource reside. It is the place of our dreams and the archetypes that order reality and give life meaning and purpose. Many people therefore conclude that this is the place where God interacts with us. Some go a step further and say that the human unconscious *is* God. The unconscious far transcends our conscious mind, guiding and empowering us in ways beyond our conscious imagining. Carl Jung believed that the human unconscious is an amalgam of a personal and a collective unconscious, of which the latter transcends us as individuals and unites us in a common spiritual reality. But whether the unconscious is all these things or not, the Christian faith denies it is God. When the human race dies the unconscious dies. God meets us in the unconscious, but is not simply the unconscious.

God is our best human construct. One way to look at the Bible, as well as the mythologies of the world, is to see it as humanity's attempt to construct God, to picture that which is ideal and which motivates us toward an ultimate healing goal. Perhaps God does not exist, but humanity still needs God for its well-being. So our task is to construct the best God that we can, that can motivate us toward the highest fulfillment, whether or not such a God exists. There is, of course, substantial truth in this description, because whenever we think about God and try to think rightly about God we are inevitably manufacturing the God we want or the God that fits within our thinking. Nevertheless, our human mental constructs should not be confused with God.

The God of the Bible is not ultimately a human construct but a divine encounter. Abraham, Moses, Elijah, Isaiah, Jesus, and Paul did not think about the concept of God and then construct an image of God; rather, within the context of their faith communities they saw visions, heard a still small voice, or in other ways had an experience of God. This was not the God of their best thinking; this was the God who swept away all of their thinking. This is the God that bursts through the purely rational and condemns the self-serving. We trust in God not because we've decided God is a good idea, but because we are in a relationship with that which is beyond us, which knows us and calls for everything in us. For some of us (such as myself) this is a subtle experience. For others it is an overwhelming numinous demand.

Pascal was a famous French mathematician and philosopher who wrote extensively on the subject of why we believe in God (one of his famous lines is, "The heart has reasons reason knows not of"). But what no one knew until after his death was that Pascal himself had an overwhelming experience of God. Sewn into his clothing was a paper he kept with him for years. It said, "In the year of grace 1654, Monday 23 November . . . from half-past ten in the evening till about half an hour after midnight: FIRE. God of Abraham, God of Isaac, God of Jacob. Not of the philosophers and the learned. Certitude. Certitude. Emotion. Joy . . . Joy! Joy! Joy! Tears of Joy . . . My God . . . let me not be separated from thee for ever." On the paper was a drawing of a blazing cross.[7]

Whatever we may think of Pascal's experience, he clearly was not constructing God. As he himself noted, this is not the God of the philosophers, not the God of human thought and rational construct; this is the God of encounter, of relationship, that pierces our deepest being. We do not simply imagine that God must be beyond us; God *is* beyond us, or God is not God.

But one might ask: Does such a God actually exist? Is such a God—originator, sustainer, lover, healer, subversive—consistent with what we know of reality through other channels? Or is such a picture of God ruled out by other information and experiences? Though we live in a society in which the vast majority say they believe in God, our culture frequently expresses doubts and disbelief as well. The reasons for doubting or disbelieving usually fall into two areas: science and suffering.

God and Science

Two hundred years ago, Pierre-Simon Laplace, one of history's greatest mathematicians and astronomers, wrote a book explaining the workings of the solar system without making any reference to God. When Napoleon Bonaparte asked him why his book failed to mention God, he supposedly replied, "Sire, I had no need of that hypothesis." This typifies the scientific method. The scientific method does not deny the existence of God, but it seeks to explain all observable phenomena without reference to supernatural causes. As a result, the more science is able to explain, the less God is needed as an explanation. But this does not mean that God is being eliminated from reality; rather, science is eliminating a false god.

7. Quoted in Borg, *God We Never Knew*, 43.

The God of the Bible and Christian faith is not an invisible force that lives in the gaps of whatever we can't explain. God is the "Wholly Other" that is present in the mundane as well as the mysterious, fully overlapping the natural world. Science is a natural explanation; religion is an existential explanation; but it's all one reality. Science asks, "How does this work?" Religion asks, "How and for what do we live?"

Einstein once wrote, "Science without religion is lame. Religion without science is blind."[8] The two realms need each other. Not only do they complement each other, but they also contribute to each other. The Christian faith has made widespread use of science in order to further its mission of bringing wholeness to the world. To cure a fever through medicine is as much the work of a Christian as to bring relief through prayer. The Christian faith welcomes increasing knowledge of the natural world because the natural world is God's world—a gift to humanity for our enjoyment, creativity, and care. Not only does science enhance the mission of the Christian faith, it also helps to improve our theology—our understanding of God—by looking more profoundly into how God's world works and the mysteries of human nature.

Science is also indebted to the Christian faith. It was the Christian faith's positive view of nature as something good—but also as something different from God—that helped provide the intellectual environment and framework necessary for the development of science in the Western world. And when science develops new technologies it is often religion that is called upon to help evaluate the proper use of that technology. Science by itself has no inherent ethic except to be truthful. It needs a partner to make science beneficial for humanity and the environment.

Some scientists believe that science ultimately points in a religious direction. For instance, at the bedrock of science rests mathematical equations that describe natural reality. But why is it that nature is describable by equations? And why is it that our brains are capable of creating and understanding those equations? And why is it that the way we judge the validity of the equations is through a particular sense of beauty and economy? And why is it that the universe actually conforms to our notions of mathematical beauty and economy? And how is it that we have evolved these brains capable of reflecting upon these wonders? As Einstein put it, "The eternal mystery of the world is its comprehensibility."[9]

8. Einstein, *Ideas and Opinions*, 46.

9. Ibid., 292.

Another astonishing quality of the universe is that it appears to be finely tuned so as to make possible the evolution of galaxies, stars, planets, and carbon-based life. If the force of the attraction between protons were only slightly different, all of the hydrogen in the Big Bang would have turned into helium, and then there would have been no galaxies and stars. If the electrical charge of the electron varied, chemistry would have been blocked. If the atomic level of the carbon atom differed by half a percent, life would have been impossible. Virtually any variation in any number of fundamental givens (for which there is no known mathematical or physical reason why they could not have been different) would have resulted in a universe quite incapable of developing any complexity. Even the size and age of our universe—with its hundred billion galaxies, each with a hundred billion stars—are needed for the eventual development of intelligent life. The odds against the Big Bang creating any universe at all—let alone a universe with organized complexity, including beings with consciousness, values, and the capacity to create meaning—are (forgive the pun) astronomical. Virtually any other mathematically and physically possible universe would have been not only lifeless, but blank.

As astonishing and (at least partially) unexplainable as our universe seems to be, I do not believe any of this makes the existence of God necessary or even probable. It just means that science has limitations. We humans can never completely understand ourselves, let alone all the rest of reality, if only because we have no point outside of ourselves from which to observe.

The scientist within me would like to know how God operates in and through natural processes in the material universe, but since science has no access to God and God is not an entity within the universe, I think this question is unanswerable and wrong-headed. Nevertheless, some have tried to answer it. They point out that the universe appears to be a complex interplay of the determined and the undetermined, of regularity and randomness, of law and chance, of preconditions and the freedom to choose. Might it be that God operates through this interplay? Many theologians have suggested models by which God could influence outcomes without violating the known processes of nature. Some argue that if God's power is the power of love then God would never impose God's will on nature, but would instead be a persuader at the various levels of nature, particularly within the choices made by human beings.

As attractive as some of these suggestions may be, I am doubtful that any model of integration between God and science can be achieved.

Knowledge of God is relational, not objective, and our knowledge of nature will always be incomplete. To make our concept of God conform to the current models of reality proposed by science is short-sighted as well as near-sighted. Let scientific models continue to develop, and let God be God.

God and Suffering

One day a woman came into my office, sat down in a chair, and said, "I don't believe in God, and I hate God." I did not point out to her the contradiction in this statement; I knew what she meant. If God is all-powerful and all-loving, as many Christians claim, then why is there such horrible suffering in the world?

Every day children are abused and murdered. Where is God when they scream for help? The long history of humans committing atrocities against other humans—torturing and tormenting and tearing apart—leaves us aghast at God's failure to provide protection or justice for the innocent. Under Nazi Germany some eleven million men, women, and children—six million of them Jews—were systematically abused and murdered in concentration camps. For many Jews and non-Jews alike the Holocaust was the end of faith in God.

The usual response of Christianity and Judaism to the trauma and tragedy caused by human cruelty is to say that such is the price of free will. God made us with the ability to choose our own behaviors and spiritual commitments. God cannot interfere with our choosing and maintain our human freedom at the same time. If we are free to love and grow then we must be free not to love and not to grow.

Surely there is truth in this answer, and yet it does not resolve all of the difficulties, let alone the anguish. Could not God have created a universe in which we can make free moral choices without the option of committing murder or causing trauma to the innocent that can never be healed? Our free will is already compromised in a variety of ways, from being programmed by our biology to our being conditioned by our social environment, so why couldn't God have tweaked our biology by making us more averse toward damaging our fellow human beings? If science were to develop the ability to edit violent tendencies out of our genetic make-up, would we implement it, viewing it as God's will to do so, or would we conclude that something essential to being human would be lost?

Humanity's free will does not explain another form of suffering—natural catastrophes and tragic accidents. A child full of joy and potential dies of brain cancer. Members of a youth group on their way to a spiritual retreat die in a car crash. A giant tsunami sweeps over a shoreline, drowning tens of thousands of people.

If God is all-loving, how could God ever want these things to happen? If God is all-powerful, why does God not prevent these things from happening? The ancient Israelites were well aware that life is often unfair and filled with tragedy. Psalm 42:3 says, "My tears have been my food day and night, while people say to me continually, 'Where is your God?'" Good people often suffer terribly while immoral people become rich and carefree. The random, senseless, and often cruel features of life led many to believe, or at least to live as if, "There is no God" (Psalm 14:1). Today many people insist that God cannot be both all-loving and all-powerful; either God cannot prevent senseless tragedy, or God will not. A God who will not is—at best—amoral, and a God who cannot is not God.

Some Christians believe that everything that happens, no matter how painful or evil or apparently accidental, has a divine purpose. Nothing happens without God willing it to happen. This does not mean that God wills evil, but God's omniscience (knowing everything) allows God to see and make use of all the consequences of all occurrences, including our own choices, so that eventually everything works together toward the best conclusion. It is impossible for us to see this bigger pattern, but our faith in God's power and love assures us that it is there. Sometimes this is pictured as a tapestry that on its underside appears disconnected, but when turned over one sees that the complexities of thread have created a beautiful whole.

Other Christians take a less deterministic view of God's action. The various accidents that happen to us are just that—accidents. God has created this world with its balance of randomness and regularities so that this world, and we humans, are free to develop. This balance is what allows for evolution, change, choice, creativity—not only for humans but for everything—and results in immense happiness and pleasure (at least for humans). But the flip side to randomness and regularity is that if you are standing under a falling tree you will be crushed. Some of your random genetic mutations will perhaps have long-term benefits for the entire species, but some of those mutations may result in cancer for you now. The randomness and regularity that enables you to choose to create a symphony also enables you to choose to send people to the gas chambers.

According to this understanding, God is at work in and through the randomness and regularities. God made it all good, as Genesis affirms, but in day-to-day living it can get very messy and painful. But even in the midst of the suffering God is at work relating to us and working through us. God suffers with us, sharing our pain and grieving through our tragedies, but God also provides resources for God's wholeness to work itself out in the midst of a still developing world. Meaningless tragedies are exactly that—meaningless. God did not will them, nor are they part of a greater plan. But God is there nonetheless, instilling in us a vision for meaning so that we become partners with God in redeeming our life together in this world.

Despite the tensions, the Christian faith experiences God as both ultimate power and ultimate love. We believe in God not because we have worked out our intellectual questions about God, or because the pain of our tragic suffering has been wiped away, but because we have experienced God in a relationship.

In the Book of Job an innocent and righteous man suffers terrible losses and physical pain. He cannot understand why God would have done this to him and he demands that God give him an answer. God comes to Job in a whirlwind and shows him mysteries of the universe that are beyond human understanding. Job receives no answer as to why he suffers, but he realizes that his relationship with God ultimately transcends his ability—or need—to know.

Do we love God, trust God, and do what is right only if we receive tangible benefits, or will we do God's will even in the face of personal suffering? Will we live for God's kingdom even if our prayers go unanswered? Will we serve God for nothing? This is the question that broods over the Book of Job, and an affirmative answer is the most profound fulfillment of loving God.

Two factors persuade me that the God I experience through the community of faith is true. The first is that gratitude and trust in God bring healing. The second is an intuition I cannot escape.

Trusting in God and participating in a religious community appear to have health benefits. One study found that, out of a random group of two thousand people, those who had attended religious services once or more each week lived on average seven years longer than those who never attended. About half of that gap in lifespan could be explained by attendees having healthier lifestyle habits (such as smoking or drinking less), but even controlling for those differences, the attendees lived years longer.[10] Other studies have found that people who are religiously active are hospitalized less often, that people who pray and read the Bible tend to have lower blood pressure, and that people who attend religious services tend to have stronger immune systems.

Religious faith and participation also seem to have benefits for personal happiness. People who have a higher degree of religious commitment usually feel better about their families, their work, and their ability to influence things in their community. Religion is often a stronger predictor of happiness than education level, income level, or occupation.

Statistical studies such as these are controversial because correlation does not necessarily mean causation, and it is impossible to control for all social, psychological, and physical variables. Nonetheless, the results of these studies correlate with my own experience of what I have witnessed in faith communities: trusting in God gives life meaning, purpose, joy, and greater well-being.

I think that part of what makes religious faith so good for us is that it gives us a firm basis for our self-esteem. If we do not believe in God, or in any transcendent absolute over nature, from where do we receive our value? Without God our value is in the hands of those around us; they determine whether we are valuable and to what degree. Our value is then contingent on pleasing others and being pragmatically useful. But what if we are severely disabled or a burden on others? What if we suffer deep shame and public humiliation? Are we then of less value as human beings? Our secular schools teach children that they are inherently valuable, but based on what? Without God there is nothing "inherent"; when we face shame or disability the thinness of secular humanism becomes apparent. But if we believe our value is God-given we are then freed from the tyranny of our self-esteem being dependent on pleasing others. There is deep mental health in Francis of Assisi's pronouncement, "Blessed is the servant who esteems himself no better when he is praised and exalted by people than when he is considered worthless, simple, and despicable; for what a man is before God, that he is and nothing more."[11]

Alcoholics Anonymous, and other twelve-step programs that it has inspired, has had uncommon success in helping the physically addicted stay sober. Certainly the social reinforcement provided by a group all striving

10. Hummer et al., "Religious Involvement and U.S. Adult Mortality," 273–85.

11. Quoted in Adels, *Wisdom of the Saints*, 130.

for sobriety is a crucial component. But there is more to it than that. The step of turning one's will and life over to a higher power is at the heart of the twelve-step program. This isn't just pious language; it appears to make an actual difference in providing the orientation needed to maintain sobriety. When people turn their will and life over to that which is greater than themselves, an internal reconfiguration takes place that has visible results.

Freud considered religion a form of psychological immaturity, a crutch. If this were true then religion, on the whole, should result in people being less emotionally mature, but this is not the case. When people participate in faith communities, and practice faith, it usually brings out healthy and happy aspects of human beings. Of course religion can be abused, and many religious communities are more sick than well. But that is not the effect of religion itself; that is the effect of the fears and self-centeredness we bring to religion. We tend to distort even good things in proportion to our own immaturity—whether that be sex, eating, playing, or practicing religion. Religion that encourages mistrust of others and hatred for self will have a negative effect on participants and on society as a whole. But healthy faith helps us grow beyond those immaturities. Religious faith, overall, moves us in the direction of greater happiness, health, productivity, creativity, and purposefulness.

Certainly it is possible to be an atheist and be perfectly happy, good, and mature. But one could argue that society as a whole is made more well by the presence of communities of faith. Since the Enlightenment there have been various attempts to create a scientific "religion" or morality, replacing religion based on transcendent encounter, but none has so far shown itself to be successful at creating an ongoing, healing community. Indeed, some atheistic philosophies, such as social Darwinism and Neitzsche's Super-Man and Marx's dialectical materialism, led to devastating results in the twentieth century, much more horrific than anything wrought by religion.

On the other hand, I do not think religions have shown themselves to be superior to secularism when it comes to wielding the power of the state. Theocracies go to war, commit atrocities, and suppress their own citizens at least as often as modern secular governments. The Christian faith, in particular, does not seem to be designed for exercising the coercive power of the state; they are incompatible ethical systems. Jesus' ethic of self-giving love is quite different from national self-interest and the use of force. When the Christian faith has been wedded with the power of the state, the result has almost always been the abandonment of Jesus' ethic and the way of the cross. The Christian faith is most true to itself when it is in the form of voluntary communities of faith that stand in distinction to the government and act as a witness to it, seeking to persuade and transform its ways. As Martin Luther King Jr. put it, "The church . . . is not the master or servant of the state, but rather the conscience of the state. It must be the guide and critic of the state, and never its tool."[12]

Do the social and health benefits of religion prove that God is true? No. It may be that faith in God is demonstrably good for us and yet there be no such thing as God. And yet this seems unlikely to me. Even science operates from a pragmatic premise that if it works it's as good as true. Science is unable to see directly ultimate material reality, but it creates models of reality that explain most of the data. If the models work, if the equations result in a rocket successfully passing by Pluto for close-up photos, then it is as good as true—as close to reality as we're going to get. Similarly, if religion models an experienced spiritual reality that produces good results, then it is as good as true—as close to reality as we're going to get. If there truly is no God then one would expect that a philosophy of principled atheism would result in consistently healthier, more productive people. But this does not seem to be the case. When faith in God is so clearly good for us in such a broad range of ways, one suspects that it rests on a deep well of truth.

The second factor that persuades me that God is true is intuition—not just my intuition, but humanity's in general. Every culture throughout history has had some sort of belief in God or gods or a power that is greater than ourselves or the immediate world of sensation. Belief—and awareness—of God is built into us. Brain research has indicated that there is a portion of the brain responsible for religious faith. We are truly "hardwired" for faith. As Augustine famously wrote, "You have formed us for yourself, and our hearts are restless until they find rest in you."[13]

Of course, having a biological inclination to believe in God does not mean God is true. But the same evolutionary process that gave us brains that could intuit the mathematical truthfulness underlying the physical universe gave us at the same time this awareness of the transcendent Other. Just as we have an intuitive sense that knows the universe must be comprehensible and conformable to our thought, so we have an intuitive sense that knows there is transcendent meaning and purpose. Both intuitions have

12. Quoted in Yancey, *What's So Amazing About Grace?*, 238.
13. Augustine, *Confessiones* 1.1.

made us the human beings we are today, and this second intuition has been a major force behind our art, music, and morality.

What if we were to deny our intuition of God? What are the implications of concluding that only material reality is true? If materialism represents the ultimate reality—if there is no God and all that exists is matter and energy interacting randomly—then we are forced to conclude that there is no reason for life, no purpose or meaning in the universe, and that such things as justice, love, goodness, and beauty have no absolute reality. With some mental effort we can hold such a position abstractly in our heads, but we can't sustain it in the way we live. It is an untenable position for human life. It is quite impossible for humanity to function with a strictly scientific, material view of reality. We know that cannot be all there is to reality because the reality we know within us is so much larger.

Our intuitive, inescapable knowledge that reality is far more than material reductionism, combined with the experience and evidence that faith in God is so broadly good for us, makes (for me at least) a persuasive basis for trusting in the God we have encountered through communities of faith.

When push comes to shove, we cannot help but be spiritual. Even atheists are, in a sense, spiritual—often attributing to nature a quasi-mystical quality, and dreaming for something science, by itself, cannot deliver. Everyone lives by faith in something beyond blind materialism. Our passion—a life worth living—requires commitments to those things that cannot be proven or known objectively. The best life—the only human life—is lived by faith.

Is there a God? Perhaps we can identify with Simone Weil, who wrote, "A case of contradictories which are true. God exists: God does not exist. Where is the problem? I am quite sure that there is a God in the sense that I am quite sure that my love is not illusory. I am quite sure there is not a God in the sense that I am quite sure nothing real can be anything like what I am able to conceive when I pronounce this word."[14]

I sometimes imagine someone asking me, "Do you believe in God?" I answer, "No, but I trust in God." I do not give ultimate credence to my mental constructs, but I do strive to rest in, rely upon, and live for that which is good and always loves. And that, I think, is what matters.

In the Christian community of faith I have found a story being lived out that brings great joy and wholeness to life. It has become my story through

14. Weil, *Gravity and Grace*, 103.

which I encounter God, the ground of all being. In Jesus, the climax of the story, I find the most profound metaphor for God, a God who gives me grace, assures me of hope, and leads me and the community on the way to wholeness. I give my life to this God, and when I do I become my truest and best self.

Acknowledgements

This book is the culmination of nearly fifty-five years of experiencing and thinking about Christian faith and community. No faith community has shaped me more than the one that nurtured me during the first decades of my life: Lombard Mennonite Church. The rich memories of our life together continue to guide me. I am deeply indebted to other congregations as well: Dunlap United Methodist Church, where I experienced a ministry of pure grace; Peoria-North Mennonite Church, where we created a diverse expression of the kingdom of God; First Mennonite Church in Indianapolis, where I raised my children and matured as a pastor; and First Mennonite Church of Richmond, where I have the honor of currently serving.

I have had the good fortune of being mentored by extraordinary pastors: Leroy Kennel, E. Joe Richards, Emma Richards, Curt Sylvester, and Ivan Kauffmann. Of the many pastoral colleagues who have helped make ministry delightful and creative, I especially want to recognize Randy Roth, Chris Bowman, John Koppitch, and Shannon Walker Dycus. I could share anything with them.

I also need to acknowledge my debt to the scholars, writers, and teachers who have profoundly influenced my understanding and practice of the Christian faith, and whose insights and inspiration reside behind many of the words in this book. In particular I should mention John Howard Yoder, Gordon Kaufman, David Augsburger, Dennis MacDonald, Marcus Borg, John Shea, E. P. Sanders, John Dominic Crossan, Dale Allison, Luke Timothy Johnson, Phyllis Trible, A. K. M. Adam, Ian Barbour, John Polkinghorne, Richard Foster, David Steindl-Rast, Howard Clinebell, Harold Kushner, Huston Smith, Lesslie Newbigin, and C. S. Lewis.

Early in my pastoral ministry I became a volunteer counselor at the Chemical Dependency Center at Proctor Hospital. What I learned from the counselors and patients about addiction and the twelve-step program of Alcoholics Anonymous gave me a powerful lens through which to see the Christian faith. The insights I gained there undergird much of this book.

In 2008 I received a grant from the Lilly Endowment Clergy Renewal Program, which allowed me to take a summer sabbatical. I spent part of that time in a cabin in Alaska writing the first draft of this book. When I returned to my congregation in Indianapolis a weekly class read and discussed the manuscript, giving me valuable feedback and making this book a communal effort. Many drafts over many years followed. Three readers in particular helped me through detailed written critiques and suggestions: J. Daniel Hess, Shari Wagner, and Tom Kreider.

This book is meant to describe and foster healing communities; it is also the result of them. Thanks to you all.

Bibliography

Adels, Jill Haak, ed. *The Wisdom of the Saints: An Anthology*. New York: Oxford University Press, 1987.

Adam, A. K. M. *Faithful Interpretation: Reading the Bible in a Postmodern World*. Minneapolis: Fortress, 2006.

Allison, Dale C. *Constructing Jesus: Memory, Imagination, and History*. Grand Rapids: Baker Academic, 2010.

————. *The Historical Christ and the Theological Jesus*. Grand Rapids: Eerdmans, 2009.

————. *Resurrecting Jesus: The Earliest Christian Tradition and Its Interpreters*. New York: T. & T. Clark, 2005.

Ammerman, Nancy Tatom. *Congregation and Community*. New Brunswick, NJ: Rutgers University Press, 1997.

————. *Pillars of Fire: American Congregations and Their Partners*. Berkeley: University of California Press, 2005.

Armstrong, Karen. *The Case for God*. New York: Knopf, 2009.

Aslan, Reza. *Zealot: The Life and Times of Jesus of Nazareth*. New York: Random House, 2013.

Augsburger, David. *Caring Enough to Confront: How to Understand and Express Your Deepest Feelings toward Others*. Ventura, CA: Regal, 1981.

————. *Caring Enough to Forgive / Caring Enough to Not Forgive*. Scottdale, PA: Herald, 1981.

Barbour, Ian. *Religion in an Age of Science*. Vol 1. San Francisco: HarperSanFrancisco, 1990.

————. *When Science Meets Religion: Enemies, Strangers, or Partners?* San Francisco: HarperSanFrancisco, 2000.

Barr, Stephen M. *Modern Physics and Ancient Faith*. Notre Dame: University of Notre Dame Press, 2003.

Bausch, William J. *Storytelling: Imagination and Faith*. Mystic, CT: Twenty-Third, 1984.

Berger, Peter L. *A Rumor of Angels: Modern Society and the Rediscovery of the Supernatural*. Garden City, NY: Anchor, 1969.

Borg, Marcus. *The God We Never Knew: Beyond Dogmatic Religion to a More Authentic Contemporary Faith*. San Francisco: HarperSanFrancisco, 1997.

————. *Jesus: Uncovering the Life, Teachings, and Relevance of a Religious Revolutionary*. New York: HarperOne, 2006.

Bibliography

————. *Meeting Jesus Again for the First Time: The Historical Jesus and the Heart of Contemporary Faith.* New York: HarperCollins, 1994.

Borg, Marcus, and N. T. Wright. *The Meaning of Jesus: Two Visions.* New York: HarperOne, 1999.

Buxham, Yitzhak. *The Light and Fire of the Baal Shem Tov.* New York: Continuum, 2006.

Campbell, Joseph. *Myths to Live By: How We Re-Create Ancient Legends in Our Daily Lives to Release Human Potential.* New York, Bantam, 1972.

Carey, George. *Why I Believe in a Personal God: The Credibility of Faith in a Doubting Age.* Wheaton, IL: Shaw, 1989.

Chilton, Bruce. *Rabbi Jesus: An Intimate Biography.* New York: Image, 2000.

Clinebell, Howard, Jr. *Mental Health through Christian Community: The Local Church's Ministry of Growth and Healing.* Nashville: Abingdon, 1965.

Crossan, John Dominic. *The Dark Interval: Towards a Theology of Story.* Sonoma, CA: Polebridge, 1988.

————. *In Parables: The Challenge of the Historical Jesus.* New York: Harper & Row, 1973

————. *Jesus: A Revolutionary Biography.* San Francisco: HarperSanFrancisco, 1994.

Crossan, John Dominic, and N. T. Wright. *The Resurrection of Jesus: John Dominic Crossan and N. T. Wright in Dialogue.* Minneapolis: Fortress, 2006.

Davies, Paul. *The Mind of God: The Scientific Basis for a Rational World.* New York: Touchstone, 1992.

Davis, Stephen, Daniel Kendall, and Gerald O'Collins, eds. *The Resurrection.* New York: Oxford University Press, 1998.

Dawn, Marva. *Morning by Morning.* Grand Rapids: Eerdmans, 2001.

De Gruchy, John W. *Led into Mystery: Faith Seeking Answers in Life and Death.* London: SCM, 2013.

Dorrien, Gary. *The Making of American Liberal Theology: Crisis, Irony, & Postmodernity 1950–2005.* Louisville: Westminster John Knox, 2006.

————. *The Word as True Myth: Interpreting Modern Theology.* Louisville: Westminster John Knox, 1997.

Eagleton, Terry. *Culture and the Death of God.* New Haven, CT: Yale University Press, 2015.

Ehrman, Bart D. *Jesus: Apocalyptic Prophet of the New Millennium.* Oxford: Oxford University Press, 1999.

Einstein, Albert. *Ideas and Opinions.* Translated by Sonja Bargmann. New York: Bonanza, 1954.

Eliade, Mircea. *The Myth of the Eternal Return: Or, Cosmos and History.* Princeton, NJ: Princeton University Press, 1971.

Epperly, Bruce G. *Process Theology: A Guide for the Perplexed.* New York: T. & T. Clark, 2011.

Foster, Richard J. *Celebration of Discipline: The Path to Spiritual Growth.* San Francisco: Harper & Row, 1978.

Frankel, Viktor E. *Man's Search for Meaning.* New York: Washington Square, 1985.

Fredricksen, Paula. *Jesus of Nazareth, King of the Jews: A Jewish Life and the Emergence of Christianity.* New York: Knopf, 1999.

Funk, Robert W., Roy W. Hoover, and the Jesus Seminar. *The Acts of Jesus: The Search for the Authentic Deeds of Jesus.* New York: Polebridge, 1988.

————. *The Five Gospels: The Search for the Authentic Words of Jesus.* New York: Polebridge, 1993.

Bibliography

Galindo, Israel. *The Hidden Lives of Congregations: Discerning Church Dynamics.* Herndon, VA: Alban Institute, 2004.

Gordon, Ernest. *To End All Wars.* Grand Rapids: Zondervan, 2002.

Grant, Robert M., with David Tracy. *A Short History of the Interpretation of the Bible.* Minneapolis, Fortress, 1984.

Hall, Douglas John. *What Christianity Is Not: An Exercise in "Negative" Theology.* Eugene, OR: Cascade, 2013.

Halpem, Baruch. *The First Historians: The Hebrew Bible and History.* University Park, PA: Pennsylvania State University Press, 1988.

Hanh, Thich Nhat. *Peace Is Every Step: The Path of Mindfulness in Everyday Life.* New York: Bantam, 1991.

Harvey, Van A. *The Historian and the Believer: A Confrontation Between the Modern Historian's Principles of Judgment and the Christian's Will-to-Believe.* New York, Macmillan, 1969.

Horden, William E. *A Layman's Guide to Protestant Theology.* New York: Macmillan, 1968.

Hummer, Robert A., Richard G. Rodgers, Charles B. Nam, and Christopher G. Ellison. "Religious Involvement and U.S. Adult Mortality." *Demography* 36/2 (May 1999) 273–85.

Jackson, Gordon S., ed. *Quotes for the Journey: Wisdom for the Way.* Eugene, OR: Wipf & Stock, 2009.

Kaufman, Gordon D. *Jesus and Creativity.* Minneapolis: Fortress, 2006.

Kelber, Werner H. *Mark's Story of Jesus.* Philadelphia: Fortress, 1979.

Kraus, C. Norman. *The Community of the Spirit.* Grand Rapids: Eerdmans, 1974.

———. *Jesus Christ Our Lord: Christology from a Disciple's Perspective.* Scottdale, PA: Herald, 1987.

Kraybill, Donald B. *The Upside Down Kingdom.* Scottdale, PA: Herald, 1978.

Kung, Hans. *Does God Exist?: An Answer for Today.* Farmington Hills, MI: Greenhaven, 1981.

Kushner, Harold. *When Bad Things Happen to Good People.* New York: Avon, 1981.

———. *Who Needs God?* New York: Pocket, 1989.

Lapide, Pinchas. *The Resurrection of Jesus: A Jewish Perspective.* Translated by Wilhelm C. Linss. Eugene, OR: Wipf & Stock, 1982.

Le Donne, Anthony. *Historical Jesus: What Can We Know and How Can We Know It?* Grand Rapids: Eerdmans, 2011.

Lewis, C. S. *The Great Divorce.* New York: HarperOne, 2015.

———. *Mere Christianity.* Westwood, NJ: Barbour, 1952.

Liechty, Daniel. *Theology in Postliberal Perspective.* Philadelphia: Trinity, 1990.

Marxen, Willi. *Jesus and Easter: Did God Raise the Historical Jesus from the Dead?* Nashville: Abingdon, 1990.

McAdams, Dan P. *Stories We Live By: Personal Myths and the Making of the Self.* New York: Morrow, 1993

Meier, John. *A Marginal Jew: Rethinking the Historical Jesus.* Vols. 1–2. New York: Doubleday, 1991, 1994.

Mifflin, Lawrie. "A Portrait of Power and Grace." *New York Times,* August 12, 1984. http://www.nytimes.com/packages/html/sports/year_in_sports/08.12.html.

Morris, Thomas V., ed. *God and the Philosophers: The Reconciliation of Faith and Reason.* New York: Oxford University Press, 1994.

Moyers, Bill. "Introduction." In *The Power of Myth*, by Joseph Campbell with Bill Moyers, xi–xx. New York: Anchor, 1988.

Murphy, Nancey, and George F. R. Ellis. *On the Moral Nature of the Universe: Theology, Cosmology, and Ethics.* Minneapolis: Fortress, 1996.

Newbigin, Lesslie. "The Gospel Among Religions." In *Mission Trends No. 5*, edited by Gerald H. Anderson and Thomas F. Stransky, 3–19. New York: Paulist, 1981.

Oden, Thomas C., ed. *Parables of Kierkegaard.* Princeton, NJ: Princeton University Press, 1978.

Peck, M. Scott. *The Road Less Traveled: A New Psychology of Love, Traditional Values, and Spiritual Growth.* New York, Touchstone, 1978.

Polkinghorne, John. *Belief in God in an Age of Science.* New Haven, CT: Yale University Press, 1998.

———. *Science and Theology: An Introduction.* Minneapolis: Fortress, 1998.

Robinson, James M. "The Real Jesus of the Sayings Gospel Q." *Princeton Seminary Bulletin* 18/2 (1997) 135–51.

Rollins, Peter. *How (Not) to Speak of God.* Brewster, MA: Paraclete, 2006.

Russell, Gerard. *Heirs to Forgotten Kingdoms: Journeys into the Disappearing Religions of the Middle East.* New York: Basic, 2014.

Sacks, Jonathan. *To Heal a Fractured World: The Ethics of Responsibility.* New York: Schocken, 2005.

Samuelson, Scott. *The Deepest Human Life: An Introduction to Philosophy for Everyone.* Chicago: University of Chicago Press, 2014.

Sanders, E. P. *The Historical Figure of Jesus.* New York: Penguin, 1993.

———. *Paul.* New York: Oxford University Press, 1991.

Scott, Bernard Brandon. *The Trouble with Resurrection: From Paul to the Fourth Gospel.* Salem, OR: Polebridge, 2010.

Shea, John. *An Experience Named Spirit.* Allen, TX: ThomasMoore, 1983.

———. *Stories of Faith.* Chicago: ThomasMoore, 1980.

———. *Stories of God: An Unauthorized Biography.* Allen, TX: ThomasMoore, 1978.

Sheean, Thomas. *The First Coming: How the Kingdom of God Became Christianity.* New York: Random House, 2003.

Smith, Huston. *Why Religion Matters: The Fate of the Human Spirit in an Age of Disbelief.* San Francisco: HarperSanFrancisco, 2001.

———. *The World's Religions: Our Great Wisdom Traditions.* San Francisco: HarperSanFrancisco, 1991.

Spufford, Francis. *Unapologetic: Why Despite Everything, Christianity Can Still Make Surprising Emotional Sense.* New York: HarperOne, 2013.

Stacey, David. *Interpreting the Bible.* New York: Hawthorn, 1977.

Steindl-Rast, David. *Gratefulness, the Heart of Prayer: An Approach to Life in Fullness.* New York: Paulist, 1984.

Steinmetz, David. *Taking the Long View: Christian Theology in Historical Perspective.* New York: Oxford University Press, 2011.

Stewart, Brian. "Christians Are on the Front Lines of Compassion." Address at the 160th convocation at Knox College, May 13, 2004. http://www.reformedevangelism.com/library/library03-article-cbc.html.

Swinburne, Richard. *Is There a God?* New York: Oxford University Press, 1996.

Tasto, Maria. *The Transforming Power of Lectio Divina: How to Pray with Scripture.* New London, CT: Twenty-Third, 2013.

Theissen, Gerd, and Annette Merz. *The Historical Jesus: A Comprehensive Guide.* Minneapolis: Fortress, 1996.

Tipler, Frank S. *The Physics of Immortality: Modern Cosmology, God, and the Resurrection of the Dead.* New York: Anchor, 1994.

Trible, Phyllis. *God and the Rhetoric of Sexuality.* Overtures to Biblical Theology. Philadelphia: Fortress, 1986.

———. *Texts of Terror: Literary-Feminist Readings of Biblical Narratives.* Overtures to Biblical Theology. Philadelphia: Fortress, 1984.

Tutu, Desmond, and Mpho Tutu. *The Book of Forgiving: The Fourfold Path for Healing Ourselves and Our World.* New York: HarperOne, 2014.

Vermes, Gerza. *The Changing Faces of Jesus.* New York: Compass, 2000.

Ward, Keith. *The Big Questions in Science and Religion.* West Conshohocken, PA: Templeton, 2008.

Weil, Simone. *Gravity and Grace.* Translated by Emma Craufurd. London: Routledge, 1995.

White, Heath. *Post-Modernism 101: A First Course for the Curious Christian.* Grand Rapids: Brazos, 2006.

Widemark, Sue. "Lessons from the Geese: Who Is the Author and Is It Scientifically Sound?" 2009. http://www.suewidemark.com/lessonsgeese.htm.

Wiebe, Phillip H. *Visions of Jesus: Direct Encounters from the New Testament to Today.* New York: Oxford University Press, 1997.

Wiesel, Elie. *Night.* New York: Bantam, 1982.

Wilson, A. N. *God's Funeral: A Biography of Faith and Doubt in Western Civilization.* New York: Balantine, 1999.

Wolpe, David. "Viewpoint: The Limitations of Being 'Spiritual but Not Religious.'" *Time*, March 21, 2013. http://www.ideas.time.com/2013/03/21/viewpoint.the-problem-with-being-spiritual-but-not-religious/.

Wright, N. T. *The Resurrection of the Son of God.* Minneapolis: Fortress, 2003.

Yancey, Philip, *Disappointment with God.* Grand Rapids: Zondervan, 1997.

———. *What's So Amazing about Grace?* Grand Rapids: Zondervan, 2002.

Yoder, John Howard. *Body Politics: Five Practices of the Christian Community Before a Watching World.* Scottdale, PA: Herald, 2003.

———. *Christology and Theological Method: Preface to Theology.* Grand Rapids: Baker, 2012.

———. *The Politics of Jesus.* Grand Rapids: Eerdmans, 1972.